My Start-Up Life

JB JOSSEY-BASS

My Start-Up Life

What a (Very) Young CEO Learned on His Journey Through Silicon Valley

Ben Casnocha

Foreword by
Marc Benioff

John Wiley & Sons, Inc.

Published by Jossey-Bass
A Wiley Imprint
989 Market Street, San Francisco, CA 94103-1741   www.josseybass.com

Library of Congress Cataloging-in-Publication Data

Casnocha, Ben.
    My start-up life : what a (very) young CEO learned on his journey through Silicon Valley / Ben Casnocha ; foreword by Marc Benioff.
        p. cm.
    Includes bibliographical references.
    ISBN-13: 978-0-7879-9613-0 (cloth)
    1. Comcate (Firm) 2. Internet software industry—United States. 3. Computer software industry—United States. 4. New business enterprises—United States—Management.
    5. Entrepreneurship—United States. I. Title.
    HD9696.65.U64C663 2007
    338.7'6005376092—dc22
    [B]   2007007866

Printed in the United States of America
FIRST EDITION
HB Printing   10 9 8 7 6 5 4 3 2 1

Disclaimer

This book contains true narratives based on the life of the author. Some of the events are composites of several actual events. In order to protect trade secrets, corporate relationships, and personal life histories, the names of some organizations, clients, and individuals described in this book have been changed.

Contents

Foreword   xi

    By Marc Benioff

Introduction   1

1.0   My Dot-Com Life Begins   5

    Brainstorm: Who Knows What Could Happen If You   7
Raise Your Hand?

    Brain Trust: Take Responsibility, by Heidi Roizen   11

2.0   Nature or Nurture? A San Francisco Upbringing   14

    Brainstorm: All the Fuss About "Passion"—and How   16
to Tap into Yours

3.0   The First Axiom of Business: Find a Need and   18
Fill It

    Brainstorm: The Fringe-Thoughts List: Where Most   19
Great Ideas Develop

    Brainstorm: Feedback, Feedback, Feedback   22

4.0   Comcate Is Born: The Nuts and Bolts of   26
Starting a Business

    Brainstorm: The Business Plan Myth   28

    Brainstorm: Why Some People Get More Stuff Done   33
(and Start Real Businesses)

5.0   First Meeting with a VC (It's All About the Network)   36

    Brainstorm: The Power of Mentors   37

    Brainstorm: When to Ask a Dumb Question   40

    Brain Trust: Taking Mentor Relationships to the   42
Next Level, by Brad Feld

6.0   Signing Up Early Customers: Selling the Sizzle   44
and the Steak

    Brainstorm: Asking Questions: There's a Right and   47
a Wrong Way

Brainstorm: I Have a Strategic Plan. It's Called Doing Things.   49

7.0   Confronting Failure . . . and Bouncing Back   52

Brainstorm: Building Resilience—A Transferable Quotient   57

Brainstorm: How to Create and Leverage an Advisory Board   60

8.0   Hiring an Interim CEO: My First Big Mistake   64

Brainstorm: Three Sure Ways to Maximize Luck   68

9.0   The Hunt for a COO: Recruiting a Top Team   70

Brainstorm: The Art of Courtship   78

Brainstorm: How to Overcome Fear of Failure   85

10.0   Life as a Road Warrior: Making Memorable Sales Pitches   90

Brainstorm: Presentations—Worthy of Obsession   93

Brainstorm: Pricing in an Early-Stage Company   100

Brain Trust: Life Is a Sales Call, by Jeff Parker   105

11.0   I'm a Sophomore: Balancing Work, School, and Life   106

Brainstorm: Redefining the Entrepreneurial Lifestyle: Sleep, Nutrition, Exercise   108

Brainstorm: Being a Corporate Athlete   114

Brain Trust: A Life That Works, by Chris Yeh   119

12.0   A Silicon Valley Life: Building Me, Inc.   121

Brainstorm: Networking 101   124

Brainstorm: Networking 202   126

Brainstorm: Every Cold Call Can Be Warm— Rich First-Time Interactions   128

Brainstorm: Creating and Projecting Brand "Me"   131

13.0   The Product Development Process: Cheap, Good, or Fast?   137

Brainstorm: Dare to Be Mediocre: Good Is the Enemy of Perfect   141

14.0   It's a Frugal, Frugal World: Bootstrapping Through the Inevitable Cash Squeeze   144

Brainstorm: Asking for Money Versus Asking for Advice   147

15.0 The Long, Hard Slog: Achieving Scale 149

Brainstorm: A Relationship-Based First Business 152

Brainstorm: Getting More Good Revenue and Less 154
Bad Revenue

Brain Trust: Keep Slogging Away, by Carol Rutlen 157

16.0 Fulfilling the Mission, One Customer at a Time 158

Brainstorm: Make Meaning: What Gets You and Your 160
Employees Up Each Day?

17.0 The Road Ahead: Leaders of the Flat World 162

Brain Trust: How to Think About the Future, 165
by Sean Ness

18.0 What Will You Be Shouting When You Reach 167
the Grave?

Brainstorm: Entrepreneurs Are Optimists 170

Brain Trust: Let Your Heart Guide You, 171
by Timothy J. Taylor

Appendix A: What's Next 173

Appendix B: A One-a-Day, One-Month Plan to 175
Becoming a Better Entrepreneur

Appendix C: Ben's Reading List 179

Acknowledgments 183

Endnotes 185

The Author 189

Foreword

By Marc Benioff
Founder, Chairman, and CEO, Salesforce.com

There's a revolution going on in business today. Thanks to new technologies, and especially the internet, we are living in a time when creative people can start and build their own businesses more easily and more efficiently than ever before. The entrepreneurial companies spawned in the past decade have become the power behind older and bigger corporations and have changed the way traditional organizations operate. The services these companies provide have also dramatically changed how we live. Think about the many new ways the Web allows us to communicate, make purchases, search for information, or even scope out dates.

The ability to pursue entrepreneurship and entrepreneurs themselves—from John D. Rockefeller to William H. Gates—have always given the United States a competitive edge. And now, we are enjoying a Golden Age of entrepreneurship: forty-five million Americans (30 percent of the workforce) run their own businesses; more than half of all university graduates will start a business in their lifetimes; and most of the nation's job growth and new technologies hail from entrepreneurial companies. In a report to the president on small business and the economy, William Baumol, professor of economics and academic director of the Berkeley Center for Entrepreneurial Studies at New York University, calls entrepreneurship the "indispensable component" of growth and prosperity.

The amazing thing about this "indispensable component" boosting the economy and bettering society is that it comes down to individual people. These individuals need not come from privileged backgrounds nor graduate from top universities (or any university for that matter). They are people who work hard, have good ideas, and are committed to making a difference. They are people like Ben Casnocha, people like me, and people like you.

>>

I first met Ben Casnocha when I received an email from him a few years back. Ben introduced himself as the founder and chairman of Comcate, the leading provider of web-based software for public agencies. I was familiar with Comcate as a terrific service that successfully helps organizations improve customer service and increase staff efficiency. Comcate was also a customer of my company, salesforce.com. Ben wrote saying that he had some feedback for me. I am always eager to listen to customer insights; this has been tremendously helpful in improving our products and building our business. I was also intrigued because Ben mentioned that we had a lot in common. Both Ben and I were founders and chairmen of San Francisco–based technology companies. Both of us spoke at the same industry conferences. Both of us were passionate about philanthropy and had started corporate foundations designed to serve young people. Both of us believed in the internet's power to change the way everything is done.

Indeed, as Ben suggested, we had a lot in common. Then there was this bombshell: Ben was a fifteen-year-old high school sophomore. I knew better than to dismiss him as a kid who didn't know about business, though. Most entrepreneurs learn about business either at home or through experience—not through traditional schooling. And age? Steve Case, the founder of AOL, first got into business when he was six (selling the juice from the limes grown in his backyard). Michael Dell started a company that sold stamps to collectors when he was twelve, and later launched Dell Computers from his University of Texas dorm room. Bill Gates founded Microsoft—now the world's Number 1 software company—when he was nineteen.

I knew about the possibilities of starting and succeeding in business at a young age from personal experience as well. I created my first company, Liberty Software, when I was sixteen. My background allowed me to truly appreciate and understand Ben's unconventional story.

Reading *My Start-Up Life: What a (Very) Young CEO Learned on His Journey Through Silicon Valley* was exhilarating because it brought back so many memories of my own life as a young entrepreneur. I remember being fourteen and spending hours in RadioShack teaching myself how to use a computer. By high school, I was designing Atari computer games with titles like *Escape from Vulcan's Island* and *Crypt of the Undead*. (My grandmother wrote the music for that one.) I loved running my own business. And while I made money—enough to buy a new Toyota Supra (very cool at the time) and put myself through college—financial gain wasn't the most exciting part about being an entrepreneur. The most thrilling thing was creating something—and having a hand in something that was much bigger than me.

That sentiment, learned at Liberty Software, was one of the most important drivers in the creation of salesforce.com, which is now a publicly traded company and the leader in on-demand CRM solutions. Sure, Liberty also taught me about pricing, marketing, and listening to customers, but the biggest entrepreneurial epiphany was understanding the potential power in running a business: it could serve as a tool to change the way things were done; it could help make a difference in this world.

>>

Ben Casnocha gets that. "Starting a business/being an entrepreneur still seems like the surest bet to maximize the possibility of making a huge impact on the world," he says. Ben found there was something inefficient about the way public agencies ran their offices and he figured out a way to improve it. He had a keen sense of the marketplace and used the power of the internet to effect change. He was also creative enough to think outside the traditional boxes that define business and weave philanthropic giving into his business model by committing to donate a percentage of his company's profits, time, and equity to the community.

Ben has an uncanny understanding of our *zeitgeist* and can be counted on as predicting—and ushering in—the future. (Don't take my word for it: a conference in Paris named him one of the "twenty-five most influential people in the world of internet and politics.")

My Start-Up Life is not a how-to that will delineate how to create a successful business like Comcate with a few cookie-cutter instructions. This narrative will, however, reveal everything you need to know as you begin your entrepreneurial journey. You'll learn about everything from writing a business email to dealing with offshore contractors to the dynamics of an information economy. You'll learn about the risks Ben took: the ones that paid off (offering early customers a discount) and the ones that didn't (prematurely hiring an outsider as CEO). Most of all, you will enjoy this provocative, honest, and fun romp through an entrepreneurial achievement, which will leave you determined to embark on your own enterprising endeavor—and inspired to find your own way to make a difference.

My Start-Up Life

Introduction

I was running through Ontario International Airport in California after a series of exhausting sales pitches. Not only was I sprinting out-of-control to catch a plane, I was running without my shoes on. After putting them through the x-ray scanner I hadn't had time to shoehorn them back onto my feet. My Southwest Airlines plane was going to pull away from the gate in literally five minutes.

I ran, in stocking feet, a tan suit, and ruffled tie, sweat streaming down my fifteen-year-old body. The airport became a basketball court, my focus shifting to the thrust of my arms, the spring in my calves. The sidelines were packed with cheering fast food joints. A child sitting at another gate encouragingly yelled, "Run, run, run!" And run I did. *Nothing* was going to stop me from catching this flight.

I finally made it to the gate and jammed my oversize feet into my uncomfortable dress shoes. I'm always one size too big or small—perfect, *acceptable* fit always eludes me—and then hustled onto the plane as the very last passenger to board. The flight was packed. With no assigned seating on Southwest, I made my way back to the one available vacancy: the middle seat in the very last row. I passed aisle after aisle, bumping elbows and stepping on toes. I buckled my seat belt, turned on the air vent, and planted my head on the headrest. My eyes shut slowly and I fell asleep.

I had gotten up at 3:45 for a 6 A.M. flight. It was just another Tuesday in November, my freshman year in high school, thirty thousand feet in the air on one of my cherished "sick days."

It was just another day in my start-up life.

>>

What brought me to this place? At this time in my life? I had a crazy teacher for my Macintosh Repair elective in middle school. For our class photo, "The Mac Doctor" shaved one side of his face and head completely bald. One day, during our early morning class, he forced all students to memorize the Apple Computer "Think Different" poem. I went home and memorized the poem and watched the video ad. *The people who are crazy enough to think they can change the world are the ones who do,* the narrator intoned to images of Gandhi, Martin Luther King, Ted Turner, Albert Einstein. I watched the ad again. Then again. It moved me like no other video or movie had before. It made me want to change the world.

I didn't want to wait. And I didn't.

My efforts to impact the world have taken the form of two technology companies. My current company, Comcate, is now the leading e-government/customer service software provider to small and midsize local governments throughout the United States, with thousands of public sector employees using our products each day. This book is the story of its founding.

But it is, really, more a story about an entrepreneur and his entrepreneuring. Though the narrative focuses on launching Comcate, seen in the broadest light I hope this book can speak to what empowered individuals can achieve with the right combination of luck, opportunity, and persistence. The key, from my perspective, is to think like an entrepreneur (we'll explore what that means in the coming pages). Many people don't, because when you dream big you may fail big, too.

The main narrative tracks my story chronologically and is accompanied by two special features. First, "Brainstorms" (or sidebars) draw out key business lessons and tactics that you can apply in your own life. Second, there are "Brain Trust" mini essays from a sampling of my circle of advisors who share their often hard-earned wisdom. It is rare for such accomplished businesspeople to speak so directly about what it takes to be successful. But you should understand up front: there is no ten-step program here, or twenty "secrets to success". No magic wand. Becoming a success in business takes a lot of hard work, and a lot of luck. The drive must come from within. Your motivation can't be extrinsic rewards such as money or fame—it has to be something deeper and more meaningful than that. I've been lucky to have people help me find this intrinsic drive and sense of meaning about my work in my own life. I hope this book can serve that purpose for you, as well as provide some actionable advice. After reading, check out the companion website at www.mystartuplife.com to continue the conversation.

>>

I am fortunate in many ways: I grew up in the San Francisco Bay Area, home to some of the world's smartest business and technology practitioners; I have tremendously supportive parents; I've gone to good schools. But I want to convince you that these circumstances alone are not enough to guarantee success. I've met with entrepreneurs young and old all over the world and the common thread is a *spirit,* not a background or location. Writer Joan Didion captured the necessary spirit in the conclusion of a commencement address at the University of California, Riverside. Read these words, read this book, and then go out and make things happen!

> I'm not telling you to make the world better, because I don't think that progress is necessarily part of the package. I'm just telling you to live in it. Not just to endure it, not just to suffer it, not just to pass through it, but to live in it. To look at it. To try to get the picture. To live recklessly. To take chances. To make your own work and take pride in it. To seize the moment. And if you ask me why you should bother to do that, I could tell you that the grave's a fine and private place, but none I think do there embrace. Nor do they sing there, or write, or argue, or see the tidal bore on the Amazon, or touch their children. And that's what there is to do and get it while you can and good luck at it.

My Dot-Com Life Begins

Your vision will become clear only when you look into your heart. Who looks outside, dreams. Who looks inside, awakens.
CARL JUNG

It didn't start with a dream. It didn't start in a garage.

It didn't even start with an innovative epiphany, which are perhaps entrepreneurs' most overplayed recollections. In technology entrepreneur Jerry Kaplan's excellent memoir *Startup,* he writes that he was overwhelmed by emotion when he discovered his great idea: "This unique emotion—the modern scientific version of religious epiphany—is startling in its raw power and purity. . . . We were momentarily unable to speak. I saw Mitchell's eyes become glazed and teary."

I wish my epiphany were as primal. It wasn't, and most aren't.

\>\>

Why do we remember certain moments with perfect vividness, even though they seemed normal at the time? Sometimes it is obvious when a memory will be burned into your mind forever—championship games, weddings, and the like. I still remember what started as a routine day in the year 2000 when my sixth-grade technology teachers Paul Williams and Kirk Lorie wrote on the board our idea for a new website. I was sitting in a chair near the back wall of our computer lab. The idea seemed mildly interesting and I thought it would be a fun project for the semester. On a conscious level I didn't think twice about this "assignment." But the fact that I remember the moment with such clarity meant something inside of me knew I was about to start on a path that would change my life.

The idea was straightforward: provide a place online where citizens could vent about stuff that's broken in their neighborhood. Streetlights, potholes, tree limbs. As sixth graders, the idea grew from our collective gripes about the dirty seats at the old San Francisco 49ers stadium, Candlestick Park. The class talked about the idea for a few months but got impatient and moved on to other topics. Soon enough the semester ended. There was little material work to show for the class's efforts other than a name for the site— ComplainandResolve.com—and an agreement that talking about ideas is much easier than implementing them. We all went our separate ways after school ended.

Except me. I returned to my school's computer lab a few weeks later to roar on a high-speed internet connection (my family crawled on dial-up). It was June 2000 and dot-com mania gripped the Bay Area. I decided to open some of the Web page files from the technology class. Seeing how easy it was to create Web pages, I started spending the bulk of my days that summer working on ComplainandResolve. First, I fleshed out the idea. Allowing a place for citizens to merely vent is not enough—we would have to *help* citizens get their gripes resolved. If citizens have a complaint and either don't know who to call (and don't want to navigate government bureaucracy) or are not receiving a satisfactory resolution from their local government, they could contact us (ComplainandResolve) and we would come to their rescue. So to be of service, I thought to myself, we would have to compile a comprehensive listing of all California local government agencies. Second, we would have to bring some muscle to the matter—perhaps governments would respond to a consumer advocacy group faster than to a random citizen.

By fall of seventh grade I was readying the website and updating my parents on my activities. I needed to learn everything about operating a website, such as how to code HTML and how to register a domain name. These and other tasks took time—but more importantly—they took money. How would I fund this little activity? I opened up Microsoft Word, selected the "memo" template, and wrote a brief memo to my parents requesting $200 to start this website. More amused than anything, they complied, and I borrowed their credit card.

Brainstorm: Who Knows What Could Happen If You Raise Your Hand?

So much of entrepreneurship is simply showing up and taking small risks.

In my technology class we brainstormed a business idea but there was no follow-through. I went to the computer lab every day over the summer and turned our discussion into something real.

I showed up.

When you show up you risk embarrassment or failure. In the early days of Comcate I took many risks. I outsourced the programming of the prototype (OK decision), offered the product to early clients at a steep discount (good decision), paid an interim CEO to write a business plan (bad decision), committed to a delivery model of hosted software instead of on-site installation (probably good decision), and snuck into a couple nonvendor conferences to pitch prospects (good decision).

Today, I continue to take risks, albeit in a more calculated fashion—consider the potential upside, the potential downside, and the probability of either occurring. On my blog, I reveal personal and professional activities and leave myself open for critique—which comes in bucketloads! I travel internationally where few people speak English. At Comcate board meetings I try to advocate for the unpopular opinion.

Great entrepreneurs show up, take small risks (and sometimes, large risks), raise their hand when they're confused, and try to figure out what's going on and how a situation could be made better.

When you show up and raise your hand, you've already outperformed 90 percent of the crowd.

As my project developed, my emotions were mixed. Visions of money? Of course. Every day I'd read in the paper about the latest paper millionaire. I also liked the possibility of helping people resolve their gripes. More important, though, and I think most entrepreneurs would say this, I wanted to fix something that was broken.

>>

"You're famous," my Mom whispered in my ear, waking me one morning. The *San Francisco Chronicle,* Northern California's largest newspaper, had run a column in its business section about ComplainandResolve.com. I was stunned. Yes, I had spoken to a reporter about my activities after he caught wind of it via an online message board, but the site hadn't even launched! I was disappointed because people would presumably visit the site and it wasn't ready. But hey, it offered legitimacy. With newfound energy to get the site launched, I finished all the pages and uploaded them to a server. *Voilà!* www.ComplainandResolve.com was born.

I sat back and waited for complaints from unhappy citizens to stream in. And waited. And waited. Didn't anyone have a complaint? I was perplexed. It took me a week to figure out that I couldn't just sit on my ass once the site was up. (My role models at the time were other dot-coms that embraced the "build-it-and-they-will-come" philosophy.) Since the *Chronicle* article seemed nice, I decided to cook up some press releases using templates I found in books at the public library. After running drafts by my Dad, I sent them to a few local TV stations with the headline "Twelve-Year-Old Launches Major Citizen Complaint Dot-Com." Three weeks later, despite my having done nothing but build a website and send out several grand press releases, two teams of cameras followed my every move at school. You gotta do what it takes to attract attention to your company!

>>

I had never done a TV interview before. The night before these local TV stations joined me in my bedroom for the one-on-one, Dad schlepped out the old video camera and did a practice run. With the camera rolling, he lobbed some questions at me: "Where will ComplainandResolve.com expand to next, after California?" I responded: "Well, that's a good question. We're probably going to head south, along the coast of Latin America, and then work our way inland to countries like Paraguay and Brazil." Once Dad realized I was joking, I started laughing. The real thing actually went pretty well, except when the reporter asked a question about my company's "overhead," a foreign business term. I looked at the pro-

ducer quizzically and we moved on. The camera eye glared men-
acingly only once. A South Bay news station apparently wanted to
explore the story line of an isolated kid chained to his computer.
After zooming the lens out my bedroom window to the kids playing in the park across the street and dubbing in sounds of children
laughing, the camera came back to me. The question: "Do you feel
like you're missing *out* on your childhood?" A little taken aback, I
burst out, "But I've read all the Harry Potter books! And look at all
those sports trophies I have!"

I would have more serious and higher-stakes media experiences later on, but at the time I knew only one thing: you simply
cannot beat free media.

>>

The local press coverage generated several complaints a day. Citizens from across the state wrote in about local problems. Consulting my four-hundred-page "Book of Authorities," a compilation I
created of every phone number of every department of every local
government in California, I would phone the appropriate local government unit and be silent on the line while my Dad or Mom did
the talking. When you're young it is hard to communicate professionally with adults—let alone government officials—so this was
key learning time for me. After the call, I would email the citizen
an update.

Eventually I was able to make calls myself to the local governments, a nerve-racking experience to say the least. Relaying the
requests of our client wasn't hard on the phone, but the opening
and closing of a call was. In particular, how to professionally end a
voicemail. I soon memorized a few closings: "I look forward to
hearing from you soon. Thanks!" or "Thanks very much, take
care," or simply "Thanks!" Sometimes I would blow it, for after leaving my number and expressing an extra special thank you, I'd
revert to my scripted ending. So it would come out: "Thank you
very much again, Mr. Doe. Thanks!" I have since learned that this
awkwardness afflicts adults, too.

Despite mangled voicemail messages, I still established relationships with public works directors who grew accustomed to my
contacts. Local papers continued to write articles about my free
service. BayArea.com named us "Site of the Week," driving a ton

of traffic and providing me a free T-shirt. The now-defunct *Industry Standard* featured me and Amazon.com founder Jeff Bezos for the "quotes of the week." ("America is complaining more than ever, so we feel like it's a prime time to launch.") Seeing titles like "boy wonder" and "whiz kid" surprised me. All I did was build a website.

>>

To accompany this growth, I had to add a little bit of infrastructure to my fledgling business, if only to stave off embarrassment. Tom Ammiano, a well-known member of the San Francisco Board of Supervisors, once returned a call from ComplainandResolve.com himself. At that time, the phone number for ComplainandResolve doubled as my family's home phone number. My brother picked up the call and said, "Whoa, who is this? Tom who?" As far as I was concerned, having Tom Ammiano return a call personally was like Bill Gates returning a Microsoft tech support inquiry. It worked out in the end, though you can imagine the conversation (nonviolent, of course) I had with my brother afterward. After that incident I secured a toll-free voicemail number. I could never "answer" a phone call, but I would get messages and then could call them back on my home land line when I was certain my brother wasn't on the phone and my dog wasn't barking in the background.

>>

Making money didn't cross my mind until I contracted with a pay-per-click ad banner company that ran advertisements on my site. I earned a few cents every time someone clicked on an ad. I needed $20 before the company would cut a check. I had $18 when the ad banner company went out of business. Around that time a reporter for the *Oakland Tribune,* in an interview, asked me how I was making money. I didn't have a good answer, and she laughed in a slightly irritating high-pitched tone that said, "Oh, you *are* a dot-com entrepreneur." I smiled a fake smile back to her. She was right. And I was exhausted.

>>

I was happy with what I had accomplished but realized the work had become more of a chore than a joy. This is as clear a sign as any to move on. ComplainandResolve.com had established relationships with several dozen local government agencies in California and helped more than one hundred citizens resolve their issues. By this measure I considered the effort a success, despite making no money.

So that summer after seventh grade I reflected on how I had gotten engrossed in something as exciting and exhausting as my own internet company, even on a small scale. I wasn't the only one reflecting. The 1990s technology bubble had burst and there were quite a few entrepreneurs doing some serious thinking . . . only theirs was disbelief over how they could have blown through $50M in a couple years, whereas mine was whether I wanted to really be someone different or instead spend more time with school friends talking about who were the hottest girls. (If you don't remember sixth-seventh-eighth grades, this is the focus of most boy-to-boy conversations.)

By August I realized I had learned a lot about how government works and how entrepreneurs create companies. Unlike the many Americans who aren't sure how income taxes, property taxes, or traffic fines are spent, I had a growing understanding of our state and local government system. I appreciated the tireless, if sometimes inefficient, work of public servants, especially after a thirty-minute harangue from a traffic engineer who described in bloody detail how he had placed sensors under the road to time the red light exactly . . . all in response to my client's complaint.

On the business side, I learned the difference between a sole proprietorship and a corporation. I learned about client relations and marketing. I learned how to write a business letter and how to make a business phone call. On the technology side, I learned about dealing with offshore contractors. I learned about the wonders of a "flat" information economy, and how even someone as young and inexperienced as I could partake in it.

It all boiled down to one revelation: While I had learned a lot through ComplainandResolve, I was ready to move on. To what, I didn't know, but something big, something world-changing. . . .

Brain Trust: Take Responsibility

By Heidi Roizen

Three weeks into my junior year in college, my boyfriend was killed in a plane crash. It was a horrible tragedy that changed my life . . . for the better.

Certainly not because Jeff was a bad person or deserved to die in any way; in fact, he was terrific. But through his death, a harsh light was cast on my own life, and I didn't like what I saw.

Before Jeff died, I was a happily average student content to follow him after college while he pursued his passion to fly. In an instant, that plan—if you can call it a plan—was gone. I suddenly saw myself as a person who had settled for following someone else's dream, and had somewhere along the way given up my own. I was overwhelmed with not only the loss of Jeff but the loss of my own identity, which had become totally subjugated to his. I made a promise to myself: never again be dependent on another person for providing my life's meaning or direction. I took responsibility for my own life.

It has been almost thirty years since then, and just like you, I have faced many challenges. But for every one of them, I am bolstered by the conviction that I alone need to make my life work— I don't expect anyone else to chart my course, to fix my errors, to solve my problems, to make me happy. This has propelled me through some tough days, and has driven me to achieve some pretty good high points as well. This is not incompatible, by the way, with being married or having kids. I just don't count on them to give me my whole purpose in life.

About a week after Jeff died, I received his last paycheck in the mail—$60, which was twenty-five hours of labor at the time. I remember thinking, if I could only buy him back for that amount of time I would gladly pay a hundredfold more. It was a poignant marker for me of the value of each hour—what it seems worth to you when they stretch seemingly forever before you versus what you'd pay for that hour when they are scarce. Or gone. And this provided me with my second lesson from Jeff's death: part of being responsible for your life is also taking responsibility for your enjoyment of life. If you are not enjoying your life, don't blame it on someone else. Go figure out how to make it more enjoyable under your own power and on your own terms.

My hours are precious to me. I try to have a bit of fun every day—to laugh, to play. And I can speak for Ben and all the successful entrepreneurs I know: you will thrive at work when you're enjoying yourself.

So, take responsibility for each day. Don't outsource your life course. It is core to what you are going to get from and contribute to the world, so make sure you take responsibility for it yourself.

Heidi Roizen is a former entrepreneur and current influential venture capitalist in Silicon Valley. She recently served on the board of the National Venture Capital Association.

Nature or Nurture?
A San Francisco Upbringing

*No city invites the heart to come to life as San Francisco
does. Arrival in San Francisco is an experience in living.*
WILLIAM SAROYAN

It is usually around now in the story when people ask, "Wait, wait,
wait—back up. You were thirteen when this was all happening?
How and why did you pursue entrepreneurship? Why weren't you
playing baseball or doing whatever normal thirteen-year-olds do?
What are your parents telling you during all this?"

I had a rather normal childhood, devoid of the "Baby Einstein"
routines that seem to typify the twenty-first-century high-achieving
American family. My San Francisco upbringing was kind of old-
fashioned, come to think of it: lots of time outdoors, endless games
of basketball and football, family road trips through the Western
U.S., enraging (sometimes abusive) older brothers, and nonstop
silliness. Never a bored moment.

Entrepreneurship took hold early on in my life—around age
seven—but was distinctly absent from my influences. The urge to
create businesses came from within, an internal compass that—
when followed—always sets me near the right path. There's not an
entrepreneur in my family tree. My parents never said, "Ben, you
can do or be anything! Shoot for the moon!" When I was four years

old I set up a store outside my bedroom that sold magazines and other objects stolen from my parents and brothers' rooms, to which my parents responded, "Well, what are the hours of your store?" When I purchased a gumball machine that dispensed the candy at ten cents a pop, my parents didn't say, "Wow! Incredible! See how fun business can be?" Their reaction instead was dry and amused, "You're lucky your brothers have a sweet tooth!"

>>

I probably inherited an outer shell of guardedness from my Dad. He grew up with a father who traveled and was unable to attend many of his school events. His mother had no college degree. He attended an all-boys high school and all-men's college three thousand miles from home. Not surprisingly, amidst all this testosterone, he developed a streak of independence, with emotions concealed beneath a driven exterior. He, like me, discovered the life of the mind, and his talent as an expert communicator flourished in a passion for finance and law.

Despite our worldviews being quite a bit different, Mom has exerted her loving influence. She showed me how to find and clip coupons in the paper and then use them at grocery stores. She gave me books to read, got me hooked on the public library, and implored that I read the newspaper. Today, I am frugal about things that don't matter and a full-fledged bookslut.

As a child, I had different demands on my Mom than most. Most kids would ask to be picked up after soccer practice. I asked for a ride to the City of Livermore to do a sales pitch. Most kids would ask for help on their homework or organizing their schedules. I asked Mom to drop off a suit during lunch and mail Comcate tax documents. All this amounted to a professional relationship similar to the one I had with Dad.

One day my olfactory senses yanked me into the kitchen as fresh chocolate chip cookies were warming in the oven. As she baked, Mom whistled along with the classical music on the radio. I told her, casually, that the City of Menlo Park had just agreed to be a beta tester of our product. A wide smile erupted on her face. She wiped her hand off and extended it out for a firm, enthusiastic shake.

Our kind of embrace.

Brainstorm: All the Fuss About "Passion"— and How to Tap into Yours

"Find your passion and follow it," countless advice books instruct. It sounds so easy!

Nearly every college admissions application asks about your passion in life. This creates obvious heartburn for the anxious seventeen-year-old: "What if I don't know what my passions are?" A midlife crisis candidate asks a similar question, only for this person it's, "Why have I been faking this passion for so long?"

Figuring out what you love to do and then how to get paid for it is one of life's thorniest challenges. I'm lucky at a young age to have natural inclinations toward entrepreneurship and writing and I have a pretty good sense of what I'll be doing in twenty to thirty years. If this isn't you, fear not—for most people, it isn't. Just ask forty-year-olds if they predicted their current line of work when they were children.

Finding your passion is discovering what activities, causes, ideas, people, or places make you the most excited about living. Psychologist Mihaly Csikszentmihalyi calls this being in the "Flow."

The critical element of the discovery process is *exploration into the unknown*. Unless genetics pull you toward an activity, you won't find your "flow" unless you extend yourself. It's critical you travel to places you've never been to, talk to people from different walks of life, take jobs you wouldn't otherwise consider, read books on topics you're certain are not interesting. By reading a random article on the brain I discovered a genuine interest in neuroscience. By signing up on a whim for an exchange program I discovered a genuine passion for international travel. By following through on a class assignment I entered the exhilarating environment of entrepreneurship, which created the possibility to change lives, solve problems, and make money. Business became a passion, especially people-driven business that tries to make an average person's life better and easier. And I love management, the idea that people can be inspired to be and do more than they ever expected.

You must place faith in these quests for new experiences so that, somehow, new interests and unfound strengths will emerge. Trust yourself.

It's not easy. I've met people in their fifties who, when I ask why they do what they do, tell me, "My father always wanted me to be in the import/export business." Parents, advisors, teachers, and friends all make the passion-discovery process more difficult than it needs to be by trying to live their passion through you. Beware.

It is true that if you don't love what you're doing and how you're doing it, you won't be very successful at it. But don't let all the fuss about passion cause unwarranted anxiety—like the pursuit of happiness, it's a lifelong effort that rewards the open-minded.

When entrepreneurship became a passion in my life, my family offered their full, if befuddled, support. With the help of Mom, I started going to CompUSA each Sunday, armed with their newspaper advertisements offering $70 to $80 products free after rebate. I would buy all those products, send in the rebate forms, and then resell the products on eBay for slightly less than retail. This was not Mom's idea of fun, but she supported my endeavor unconditionally, sometimes driving me as far as Daly City—about a half-hour south of our home—to find the store offering the rebates.

Though I thought my rebate scheme was pretty clever—after all, $500 million in rebates go unfulfilled each year—my parents were more focused on providing the freedom and love that would allow me to pursue my evolving interests, no matter how much they diverged from their own.

And such a willingness made a huge difference . . . because before they blinked I had taken my leash of freedom to the max . . . and cut off the rope.

The First Axiom of Business: Find a Need and Fill It

There are no big problems; there are just a lot of little problems.
HENRY FORD

I celebrated ComplainandResolve.com's first anniversary by sticking a fork in it.

I wanted to start a new business using the lessons I'd learned about local government and business, so it was time to move beyond my first "practice" business, and take a shot at the big leagues.

>>

One market segment I studied had proved fertile to venture capital investment—the consumer complaint resolution space, home to companies such as PlanetFeedback.com (since acquired by Intelliseek). Consumers could submit a complaint about a company or product and PlanetFeedback would route the complaint to the appropriate parties. They made their money by offering a sophisticated suite of software tools for companies to analyze the thousands of letters consumers sent through their website.

This business model, coupled with my own experiences dealing with slow government bureaucracies, set off a spark.

Brainstorm: The Fringe-Thoughts List: Where Most Great Ideas Develop

Random ideas, quotes, people I need to talk to, a funny conversation overheard at the table next to me at my favorite café down the street, a book recommendation from a review in the paper, a gift idea, a potential blog post, a short-term task, a long-term project, and most important . . . new business ideas!

Each day dozens of fringe thoughts enter our brain. They may or may not be relevant to our main work. They materialize in various stages of development.

I try to capture, record, review, refine, and publish (on my blog) as many of these fringe thoughts as I can. Besides making you a better conversationalist, organizing your fringe thoughts is one way toward a more intellectually coherent worldview.

Among the various repositories and lists for such thoughts should be "New Business Ideas." Each time you see something that could be done better, write it down on this list. Don't be careful. Recording fringe thoughts is an exercise in creativity, and research shows that the minute we try to add a filter to our thinking—for coherence, approval, or completeness—is the minute the ideas tap goes cold.

What's on my fringe-thoughts lists? Here's a sample:

- *Business ideas.* When leaving a voicemail, press a button on your phone and it automatically records a message in your voice. ("Hey, it's Ben Casnocha, give me a call back at 415-XXX-XXXX.")
- *Long-term projects.* Take an acting class.
- *Quotes.* "Nothing is as fast as the speed of trust."—Stephen Covey

When it's time to start a new business, consult your fringe-thoughts list. It's where many great ideas germinate.

What if, instead of working for citizens to resolve their requests, we worked with *local governments* to help *them* resolve those complaints? With this breakthrough insight, I got excited, and as I do with all my ideas—no matter how half-baked—started writing about it in a Word document kept on my computer.

Over the next few weeks I studied companies that specialized in helping private businesses manage customer service. Companies mostly outsourced customer service. Some companies outsourced customer support call centers (India!), some outsourced the writing of response letters, and still others outsourced the surveying and solicitation of feedback. I looked at all these options and considered the applicability of each to the local government space. In my market research it became clear that local governments were, for the most part, completely ignored by companies targeting the private sector.

This confused me. Local governments serve hundreds of thousands of "customers," can never go out of business, and usually lag behind the private sector in implementing money-saving tech initiatives. In addition, once a local government buys your product you're usually in the door forever. This market, though, is notorious for a few things: a long sales process, occasional budget shortfalls, overworked staff, and, well, they're light-years behind the private sector so they may not be ready to buy certain cutting-edge technologies.

To confirm these assumptions and learn more about the market, I turned to my vast network of contacts—my Dad—and solicited his thoughts. He knew a local city manager, Mike Ramsey in Antioch, California, who happened to have seen a television interview with me.[1]

We set up a meeting with Mike to talk about his customer service needs.

>>

In advance of our meeting, I sent Mike Ramsey a document outlining my vision for a product to help local governments manage their citizen complaints.

---

[1] The city manager is the CEO of most U.S. city governments. The city manager reports to and is appointed by the elected city council.

On the big day, I realized I didn't own a suit, so I wore a borrowed white shirt, Mom tied my tie, and I threw a cheap second-hand blazer on top of it all. After the forty-five-minute drive we settled into his bare-walled office in Antioch City Hall. Ramsey returned the document I sent him, only this copy simmered with comments and feedback. The big news was that he loved the concept. He described cutbacks in his staff; he described how his secretary spent hours each week just routing and managing emails; he described how all city managers have a city council to please and the last thing he or a council member wanted to hear was a citizen bitch at a council meeting about an unaddressed complaint; he said he struggled to manage the expectations of his citizens in an era of Amazon.com—a service request submitted on Friday night didn't mean that a pothole would be filled on Saturday. In short, that two-hour meeting with Ramsey taught me what other entrepreneurs spend months trying to hear: a description of the problem and its ideal solution directly from the mouth of the customer, and a thorough description of the marketplace as it stands today.

The meeting with Ramsey remains among the most influential conversations of my business career. And rightfully, it was the most tiring. I still recall the exhaustion. To sit in a chair and focus intensely and act like an adult for two hours is a lot to ask of any thirteen-year-old.

>>

I cannot overstate the value in meeting with a few knowledgeable veterans right off the bat when exploring a new idea. Even if you don't have an "in" like I did through my Dad's contact, if the problem you're trying to solve is acute enough—and if you commit resources to trying to solve it—a reasonable potential customer should meet with you.

Looking back, Ramsey's viewpoint was just one in a marketplace that turned out to be full of diverse opinions. So it's important to consider how "early adopters" (innovative types who always want to be on the cutting edge) differ from "mainstream customers" (more risk-adverse and slower to act). There are usually more mainstream customers than early adopters, though you need to sign up the early adopters first.

Brainstorm: Feedback, Feedback, Feedback

When I founded Comcate I met one city manager, gained an introduction to another manager, and received an introduction from that manager to another. After building a network of potential customers, I used them as a sounding board as we developed our products. Because of detailed feedback Comcate delivered products cities found useful, instead of products dreamed up by corporate guys in an office. Obtaining feedback can simply mean the difference between success and failure.

Customer feedback is a key ingredient in any successful product development process. Get out of your office. Visit potential customers. Study the market. Talk to people. Invite critiques and criticism. Ask how you can make your idea better. Your idea will suffer if you don't.

Three warnings, though. First, be wary of accepting one anecdote as representative of an entire market. Just because one potential customer says she would like product X doesn't mean there's a meaningful market for that product. Second, sometimes customers are so ensconced in their reality that they can imagine no alternative. True innovation rarely sprouts from customer feedback, but good products must be informed by it. As Henry Ford once said, "If I had asked people what they wanted, they would have said faster horses." Third, focus groups can be effective, but know that many participants will try to impress or please the facilitator instead of offering their honest opinions.

>>

Over the next few months I focused on tasks critical to any start-up. Much of it was monotonous, tedious work. But it's all commonsense stuff that came to me naturally. First, I made a list of all the citizen service problems city managers seemed to face. At this stage there was no point trying to delineate which challenges are killers and which are just mildly painful. What *was* important was to root the list in tangible problems that the city managers, our customers, themselves dictated. Next to each problem, I noted whom it affected (that is, which person in the organization felt the pain) and how it was currently being addressed. As I better understood the market, I realized there were problems the customers didn't even know they had. But it's easiest for entrepreneurs to work with known, agreed-upon problems and promise to solve 'em better than anyone else, rather than convince a customer that they can address invisible needs.

After I created the list of local governments' citizen service problems, I outlined alternative and superior methods of address-ing them and then presented my ideas to potential customers—no easy task. No executive (or human being, for that matter) likes to admit that what he or she is doing is wrong or inefficient. There-fore, it becomes important to frame the conversation with cus-tomers in ways so *they* come to the realization that how they are currently doing business could be improved. This is easier than it sounds. Ask leading, softball questions and steer the conversations in your desired direction until the customer goes through his own process of self-discovery. You're trying to get feedback, so the point isn't to hear what you want to hear but rather to open the poten-tial customer up to a new, better way of doing something he thought was perfect.

>>

Armed with a list of problems, current solutions, and possible *bet-ter* solutions, the next step was to prioritize. I spoke with Mike Ram-sey (and some of his friends) again. "How critical are these problems?" I asked. Some problems only require "vitamins"—that is, a product that's "nice to have." Some issues require "antibiotics," which means they're mission-critical problems. Most profitable businesses solve mission-critical problems, or the "must-haves." I learned customer service is not mission-critical for organizations (whereas financial, payroll, and purchasing systems, for example, all are). My product, then, would be a vitamin. At the time I did not fully understand the challenges of trying to sell a vitamin, instead of an antibiotic.[2] This is probably because I personally had no real "needs." Like most other kids, I had wants, but I didn't

---

2 Comcate later developed products that paid for themselves. Much easier!

think about needs. Food, shelter, clothes were all taken care of by my parents. I didn't view the world through a lens of improvement, a perspective all great entrepreneurs carry.

>>

"How much would you pay for this kind of product?" I asked many city managers. This question is critical because I was trying to determine whether Ramsey's vision was a $1,000 or $10,000 product. I thought this straight-up question would be the quick and easy way to figure out how much we could charge for a product that managed local governments' citizen requests. But it was the wrong way of framing the discussion. Looking now at our average revenue per deal, our focus groups projected higher numbers than the market actually justified.

The better approach, which I wish I had taken, is to find out how much money the customer's problems are costing. For example, an employee spent one-fourth of his time routing and tracking citizen complaints, and if we could replace that employee's work, then perhaps the value of the product is one-fourth of that person's salary. It's also helpful to talk about the possible product price with specific data points from other software deals in the industry. I didn't have these data and couldn't drive the conversation in a realistic direction.

>>

Slowly but surely, the process of "finding a need and filling it" started to coalesce into a tangible product idea.

And so, one day, as I sat in my bedroom in my pajamas, reading and rereading the emails I exchanged with Ramsey and my other meeting notes, I drifted back to my first few meetings with adults—the formality, the old-person body odor, the strange jokes, all notwithstanding—and thought, "It can't be that hard; I held my own." Fortunately, I was *not* thinking about the thousands of people laid off during the dot-com bubble burst, nor was I hearing the commentators say it was the worst time to start a new business. Right then and there, I closed my eyes, took a deep breath, and said silently, "I want to start a business to solve Mike Ramsey's problem. I don't just *wanna,* I'm *gonna.* I'm going to be a real technology entrepreneur selling real stuff for money, not just a dot-com." I opened my eyes again, this deep proclamation just uttered in the risk-free but still brutally accountable world of my consciousness. I looked around in the way you listen for reindeer hooves on the roof on Christmas Eve. Nothing had changed. I was still a thirteen-year-old boy who wished his pimples would go away. And it was then that I learned a most important lesson: talk is cheap.

Comcate Is Born:
The Nuts and Bolts
of Starting a Business

*Whenever you see a successful business, someone once
made a courageous decision.*
PETER DRUCKER

Your whole life you're taught to ask for permission. A wise man
once said he prefers to ask for forgiveness.

If, before starting something, your first instinct is to ask
someone—some "authority"—for permission, then you're probably not an entrepreneur. I had no illusions about needing to be
eighteen or twenty-one to start a company. Give me a canvas so I
can start painting!

>>

Fall 2001 was winding down. What a busy few months. I had
learned a great deal about local government and my target market. Now I needed to learn about the mechanics of starting a for-
profit business. It felt similar to when my family first got internet—I
thought we only needed a Web browser. Then I learned about
Internet Service Providers.

On any given day my excitement and optimism soared or
swooned depending on the effectiveness of my self-teaching efforts.

With no entrepreneurship curriculum at school, no entrepreneurs in the family, and few programs aimed at youth, I was on my own to scour the public library, follow link after link online, and read business magazines and books. One of my favorite, more successful tactics was to monitor the business conference circuit and email speakers or presenters and request their PowerPoint presentations. Even though I didn't attend the conference, many speakers still emailed their materials. I also persuaded Golden Gate University in San Francisco to let me audit management and marketing classes for free over the summer.

When this approach worked, the results were glorious. I could search for the definition of "preferred stock" in the privacy of my own thoughts. I could research public relations and ask myself the question, "So how *do* they make toxic sludge sound good for you?" without offending someone's third cousin once removed who happens to run a small PR firm and takes pride in her work, thank you very much. I could study accounting over and over and come to enjoy acronyms like FIFO and LIFO, so long as it wasn't EBITDA, a phrase new MBAs will utter about four times a day, their starched shirts and suits unable to keep corked the smugness a six-letter acronym allows.[1]

When my self-teaching failed, I was a new kid in a big city, hungry for all of it but digesting little: I would read at length about some topic—say, the difference between "horizontal" and "vertical" markets—and then a week later hear someone use those terms in a meeting or read them in an article, and I'd feel like Pope Benedict at Rick Warren's church: it *sounds* like Christianity, but what's up with the T-shirts? There's a big difference between reading something passively and being able to apply it, describe it, analyze it, all in real time with college-educated and experienced adults. Accumulating random bits of knowledge was better than nothing, but absent real-life experiences to cohere my readings into something meaningful, I was like the A+ student who can't screw in a lightbulb. This would all change, soon, under the guidance of a mentor. Until then, the business literature accumulating on my bedside repeated one phrase over and over: "business plan."

---

1 EBITDA: Earnings before interest, taxes, depreciation, and amortization. FIFO: First in first out. LIFO: Last in first out. These last two are inventory accounting terms.

>>

In the dot-com boom there were few more popular buzzwords than "the b-plan." I'd heard absurd (but apparently true) stories of people raising $50K on nothing more than ten pages of fantasy. The covers of ad-stuffed magazines like *Entrepreneur* offered the "Five Critical Elements of Any Business Plan." To a novice, the business plan seemed pivotal, especially if you had any hopes of raising venture capital. How b-plans got so sexy is beyond me—they're just a

Brainstorm: The Business Plan Myth

The myth of business plans is that you must write a big, fat document and spend months laboring. The problem with the big, fat plan is that: (a) no one will read it, (b) it is out of date the minute you print it, and (c) you've killed too many trees. Instead, think this way:

The best business plans are short.

The best business plans are living documents.

The best business plans do more for you than for others by clarifying your own thinking.

Put pen to paper and outline the fundamentals of your business idea: the market you want to go after, the competitive landscape, your product or services, how you plan to make money, and the management team you could assemble. PowerPoint will likely constrain you. Just write in a word processor.

Then leave the office.

Talk to people. Share your ideas. Get feedback. Don't worry about confidentiality too much—other people have probably already thought of the idea, and no VC will sign a nondisclosure agreement.

I fell for the business plan myth when I started Comcate and I lost valuable time and expended unnecessary energy. Avoid this trap!

document, and I know now they are almost always out of date within five minutes of writing. But I was just a babe, so I jumped in in my birthday suit.

I spent an entire weekend sitting on a couch in our living room with the music tuned to my favorite radio station, feet on the coffee table, laptop on my legs, a glass of chardonnay sparkling on the side. . . . OK, no wine, but I felt cozy. Writing the plan raised questions that I had never considered. I was blabbing and I knew it, trying to do something big but mustering only vague sentences ("Improve customer service in local governments by developing inexpensive software"). Writing a business plan forced me to think creatively in ways different from those I'd been taught in the classroom. It wasn't enough to game the system, as we do in school, because I needed to *invent* the map to success. There was only a white screen and blinking cursor in front of me. My tools were my brain, books, and websites. Few tools and endless unanswered questions.

>>

Then manna fell, out of tragedy. My godfather Jim Edmund, the man who ignited my adoration of bow ties, had died of skin cancer. Mom, my brothers, and I heard the news while camping at Lassen National Park in California. Dad's scratchy voicemail included the date of the funeral as well as a request from Jim's wife that I speak as a surrogate son (Jim had no kids). I worked with my parents to draft a speech, mostly about fishing.

On the day of the funeral, I walked up to the podium and looked out at the somber crowd. It was my first funeral. I felt intense pressure around my sinuses—like the pain I get in my ears in airplanes during descent—and it held back tears, this pain. My brother brought out a tissue and I saw him wiping a tear off his cheek. I'm still not sure if it was a real tear or if it was him playing grown-up, since adults can always cry at the right time and in a controlled way. I, on the other hand, fiercely resisted crying for the same reason—I too wanted to play grown-up, and I felt that locking my tear ducts in place would belie age. I finished my oratory soon enough and returned to my seat in the "family" section to receive warm congratulations from my parents. I didn't crack. The next person to go up, however, did. He cried. He was at least forty. He bawled into the microphone, the gasping for air in between sobs ricocheting throughout the room. I was confused. Is this what adults did? It would not be the first time my assumptions about proper adult behavior would be challenged. It would not be the first time I foolishly fought back genuine emotion in an effort to adjust to the "politics" of an environment.

When it was all over, I took the long walk from one end of the funeral home chapel out the door. I made eye contact with the people in the other pews. All older than me, all smiling. Only a few wet cheeks. Their facial expressions seemed to say, "Good job!" I kind of nodded, though wondering why anyone would be smiling given the circumstances. The next person I made eye contact with had a special twinkle, a penetrating smile, and I gave him slightly longer eye contact of the kind you might casually direct to an attractive woman. Little did I know that this round, graying man in the pew, as much a stranger as the rest, would go on to be the most influential person in my business career.

>>

Months later, as I idled with a half-baked business plan, Dad informed me that my godfather's widowed wife Sandy had connected with one of Jim's former colleagues, Mike Patterson, then an accomplished tax partner at PricewaterhouseCoopers who worked with many start-ups and venture capitalists. He had heard me speak at the funeral, and with Sandy's encouragement, agreed to a short meeting to discuss my business idea.

All of a sudden, my half-baked business plan roared to life. I crammed in preparation for my meeting with Patterson. I reviewed the books I had accumulated on entrepreneurship and business and reedited my draft business plan. I readied my business cards. When I heard the doorbell ring, I snatched a few copies of the seven-page b-plan (the short version) from the printer and greeted Mike Patterson.

With no concept of small talk, I got started right away.

"Thanks for coming over. I have this business idea, maybe you've heard about it?"

"Yep! Sandy has told me a bit. Tell me more. I'm pretty intrigued, Ben."

"For a while now I've been working on this website that handles citizen complaints. We've gotten a bunch from California residents. I don't know, it just seems like cities need to do a better job routing, tracking, managing these inquiries, and I think software could be pretty useful." It took several years for me to assert an opinion with confidence to someone forty years my senior without excessively qualifying it with "I think" or "maybe." I wanted never to sound stupid.

Mike spent a few minutes reading the business plan and he provided me with nothing but encouragement.

"Ben, here in the Valley there are a number of retired and wealthy entrepreneurs who would love to support a kid, and the American Dream. If you can take this far enough, I can hold a cocktail party and see if they could put more money into this thing to really make it run," Mike said.

Cocktail parties? Wealthy entrepreneurs? The American Dream? Mike had been at my house for ten minutes. I was already ecstatic.

"How, exactly, does that work? I mean, what does it take to get to the cocktail party?" my Dad asked.

"Well, if you can prove that the concept could become a legitimate business, solving problems people will pay for, then these guys would put in money to help take the company to a level where VCs would be interested. They would want to install a CEO and a team because it ain't gonna get there with just Ben, but he could still stay active. They want to find a good business opportunity, but they'll also do it for Ben. Not because this one is going to be the big one, nor the company after that. It's the company after *that*. That's why they'll want to know him."

We chatted for a few more minutes.

"Well," I said. "All that seems cool, but that still seems a long way off. What do I need to do *now*? I have words on paper. . . . That's it."

"Do some P&L's and get started on the prototype," Mike said with a briskness that suggested an end to our meeting. I thought we had just gotten started, but those two tasks would keep me plenty busy, especially when I looked up what "P&L" stood for— profit and loss statement—that is, a somewhat important part of the business: how to make money!

>>

After the meeting with Mike Patterson, I was pumped to keep moving. I searched the Web to find a software programmer to code a prototype of a complaint-tracking product that reflected city manager Ramsey's vision. I had neither the skills nor inclination to try to learn how to code by myself. So I posted a sketch of the project on eLance, an online marketplace for independent contractors. Many programmers submitted bids. The highest was $31,000. The lowest was $2,200. I picked the $2,200 guy. His English name was Russell; he lived in Bangladesh.

I looked at the balance of my savings account, and then, since it had worked before, I wrote a memo to my Dad:

```
Dear David G. Casnocha,

This memo is to request $5,000 to launch a company
to be known as Comcate, as in "communicate." As you
know, the prospects for Comcate are great—there
is a demonstrated need in the marketplace, real
opportunities for angel funding, and the possibility
to develop a prototype for $2,200. The rest of this
money would be spent on sales and marketing, the
details of which to be determined later. In exchange
for your investment you would receive a considerable
number of shares of Comcate.
```

(Shares did not exist at the time.)

My Dad laughed the way parents laugh when their daughter says she wants to be president of the United States. Then he agreed. We were going to embark on this together—me in the front seat, he in the back with a watchful eye. This arrangement ultimately formed the foundation of our father-son relationship. Had he been sane and said "No," I would have plowed forward anyway. It just would have taken longer and I would have broken down my milestones into small bites. But having him onboard accelerated my plan, and I'm forever grateful.

>>

I inked the deal with the Bangladeshi programmer and over the course of the next several months exchanged more than two thousand emails with him. For a year and a half I neither spoke with Russell on the phone nor met him in person, just emails. He turned out to be perfect for what I needed—a cheap, fast programmer.

Brainstorm: Why Some People Get More Stuff Done (and Start Real Businesses)

Given two ambitious, intelligent people, both of whom have some big ideas, why does one start getting things done while the other one stays stuck in the dreaming stage? What's the difference between two people whose success is premised on executing tasks across a variety of disciplines—as is the case in most start-ups—and one seems to be able to do more quicker, while the other person spends excessive time fretting, planning, dreaming, or consulting people? Here are some differences I see:

- *People who get stuff done maintain a high commitment to themselves.* They don't want to let themselves down. The chief motivation to achieve comes from within, not externally. It is easy to *not* keep promises you make to yourself ("Gee, I think I'm going to stop smoking" or "Gee, I'm going to join the gym this month").
- *People who get stuff done strive for "good enough."* Good enough is a key principle in entrepreneurship. If your aim is "perfect," the future is so far away it may be hard to get going.
- *People who get stuff done think about the short-term future.* At the end of meetings, they ask, "So what are the next steps?" It's easy to analyze the present or dream about the distant future, but actionable tasks over the next two to four weeks are most important for keeping the ball moving.
- *People who get stuff done "dream" and "talk" as much as the next guy, but they share these dreams and ideas with others.* By sharing your intentions with others, you introduce yet another accountability mechanism.
- *People who get stuff done begin.* Taking that first step can be the hardest. Act now! As Taoism founder Lao-tzu said, "A journey of one thousand miles begins with a single step."

(Continued)

What mindset allows me to be productive? I'm fortunate not to have many onerous projects that I loathe to work on. Loving what you do is key to getting stuff done and not simply talking about it. When I'm focused on work, I take a "let's-kick-some-butt" attitude. If something is difficult, I break it down into parts and organize its related tasks on my computer. When I'm effective and productive, I treat myself by going to the gym, eating an energy bar, or making time to do a blog post.

Do you want to be known as a doer or a talker? Do you want to start businesses or just talk about starting businesses? The answers to these questions—and others like them—are better indicators of your future success in business than the slickness of your b-plan, the extent of your funding, or who you know. It's all inside *you*.

Russell built a working prototype I could show Mike Ramsey. When I met with Ramsey the next time (remember, getting face time with a potential customer is critical!) he was blown away that I had actually followed through on our initial conversations months before: "Ben, I am frankly shocked you followed up on my feedback. It's enormously gratifying to see someone act on it, and you better believe it: where you're headed is going to make connecting with our customers a whole lot easier, something I'm willing to pay for." He gave additional detailed feedback—how he wanted the application to work to suit his exact needs. I valued the specificity of his comments and promised to incorporate all of them into the product. And as I learned, businesspeople love it when you make a commitment and then follow through on it.

I was off and running.

>>

It was in eighth grade when something had to give in my increasingly busy start-up life. This something turned out to be my formal schooling, which started to slip from my radar screen. Classroom work never really returned as my central focus until junior year in high school. Although I remember some lessons from school during those intervening years, most of it is a blur. During the spring of my eighth-grade year, when Dad and I were interviewing local programmers at his law offices, I started skipping physical education—the last period of the day—to go downtown. It was during these days that something began to click for me: "I'm not normal, nor do I want to be." Formal schooling didn't make perfect sense to me. I found the real, fast-paced world of entrepreneurship more exciting than my classroom work. I found the adults I began to interact with more interesting (but less funny) than my peers at school. Even as I began slowly pulling away from the day-to-day minutia of my other teenage friends, I must have been doing something right. I later earned the top honor in my eighth-grade yearbook: "Most Popular." (I also received "Most Likely to Be U.S. President," but who cares about that?)

First Meeting with a VC (It's All About the Network)

My chief want in life is someone who shall make me do what I can.
RALPH WALDO EMERSON

For entrepreneurs, getting a meeting with a venture capitalist on the fabled Sand Hill Road, which runs through Menlo Park, and along the northern edge of the Stanford University campus, is a worthy accomplishment. If you don't know a VC personally, it can take dozens of calls and emails to secure a meeting with someone who could fund your start-up. And dozens of calls and emails are no guarantee of an audience. For me, as lady luck would have it, I met with a venture capitalist early on: my very first meeting with an adult businessperson.

>>

The value of obtaining advice from experienced people in the field is one I cherished from the start and continue to hold as essential to successful entrepreneurship. After our first introduction, Mike Patterson, my neighbor and Silicon Valley connector, offered to introduce me to businesspeople who could serve as intellectual incubators—folks who could guide me through the entrepreneurial process and become part of my nascent brain trust. The first person on his list was Greg Prow, managing director of Softbank Venture Capital (and later Mobius VC).

Brainstorm: The Power of Mentors

A famous *Harvard Business Review* article published in 1979 reported that mentored executives earned more money at a younger age, were better educated, were more likely to follow initial career goals, and had higher career satisfaction. This isn't all that surprising—experienced practitioners transferring wisdom is bound to do something!

I can't overstate the importance of mentors in my life. They have provided invaluable fellowship both personally and professionally. Personally, I have turned to wise adults on life matters—trying to make sense of my place in the world. Professionally, my mentors breathed gently on flickering embers, nurturing a wannabe entrepreneur from raw passion to smart focus. What's important in developing effective mentoring relationships?

- *Good people.* When I founded Comcate I made several visits to the Small Business Administration (SBA) of San Francisco, which provides free business coaches through its SCORE association (Service Corps of Retired Executives). These men and women have done and seen it all before—and their advice and guidance can be invaluable. And did I mention that they are *free?* Before your network is established, start easy and free! Over time, as you meet more people, don't be shy. The words, "I'm looking for mentors" is often enough. But be sure you've done loads of background research on the person. Know what makes them tick before initiating a relationship.
- *Mentors versus advisors.* There's a difference. My "advisors" tend to consult exclusively on professional-career issues whereas my "mentors" veer into personal issues. My advisors have domain expertise in an area particularly relevant to Comcate (local government or software development). The mentors I know are all over the map—entrepreneurs, teachers, poets, you name it. I think it's important to have people in both camps.

(Continued)

- *A two-way street.* The reasons mentors like to mentor is because they derive a return, too. Talk to schoolteachers and they will tell you their students teach *them* as much as they teach the students, and that they enjoy imparting their knowledge and watching it grow. The person on the receiving end of the mentoring relationship should work hard to ensure it's not totally a one-way street.
- *Diversity.* People are helpful in different ways. There are some mentors in my life who I trust particularly on issues of emotion and spirit. Others are more hardheaded analyzers who help me digest complex situations. Each brings a unique perspective to our relationship, and I have learned valuable lessons from all of them. Maintain an eclectic group of mentors to help you take on the range of issues life throws at you.

With little more than a few poorly written pages of a business plan, I was thrilled at the opportunity to meet with someone who could whip it into shape. I knew nothing about venture capital and nothing about business customs like shaking hands or making a presentation. I didn't even fully process how lucky I was to sap an hour and a half of time from a managing director of one of the world's largest venture capital firms. In all my youthful innocence, just excitement reigned.

Dad, Mike Patterson, and I drove to the Softbank offices in Mountain View. It was a splendid sunny day on the 101 freeway. It didn't take long before I saw billboards for dot-coms and technology companies, the intimidating buildings with "Siebel" plastered on the front, and the cars beside us becoming mostly BMWs and Lexuses. We weren't just going to Mountain View. We were going to the *Silicon Valley*.

>>

I didn't want to let Mike down—he had cashed in a favor for the meeting and still didn't know me well. This was a test to solidify my relationship with Mike as much as to impress Greg Prow. I was also nervous because from what I had read in newspapers, VC firms were in the dumps. The '90s tech bubble was just bursting. As we pulled into the parking lot, my palms were sweaty. But when I walked into the building out of the hot, penetrating sun I unexpectedly felt instantly transformed into a world of wealth and coolness. A secretary printed a name tag and led me to a back room where there were unlimited amounts of food and drink. Bagels, fruit platters, sodas . . . all in the kind of excess that defined this region. In fact, the red sugary buzz radiating from the donuts seemed aligned with the too-rich investors, each an expression of the other, as if being drunk on start-ups was not enough and instead every part of the building had to demonstrate irrational exuberance. Returning with my hoard, I settled in a huge, comfy chair next to Dad and Mike, picked up one of the ten business magazines on the side table, and started flipping aimlessly. The bubble hadn't burst here—yet.

Ten minutes later—VCs are *always* late to meetings—Greg lumbered down the massive silver retro staircase and greeted me with a wide smile. He had a big frame held in place by a heavily starched shirt with gold cuff links. His hair was wavy and long, but perfectly combed. We settled into expensive chairs circling a large wooden conference room table with speakerphone equipment stationed in the center. The room smelled of sugar. The walls were undecorated but snow white. I don't think we were in the chief conference room, but the fanciness still left me in a daze. I was still soaking up the ambiance—*How the fuck did I manage to pull this off?!*—when Greg announced he had detailed feedback. He had actually *read* the business plan I sent him! He went to the whiteboard and drew up numbers. That's when I started kicking for air.

Market share, channels, distribution strategy, competitive analysis, revenue run rates—all these were unfamiliar phrases that Greg used in the context of typical VC questions: "What one thing in the world will you be better at than anyone? How will your product be positioned against other products? What's the market landscape like—wide open, fragmented, dominated by IBM types, etc.? How long is the sales cycle? How do local governments buy? What channels do they use? How good is the technology?" It wasn't grilling. After all, I wasn't trying to raise money (just get feedback) and I was, well, a kid. There was no wrong answer. Greg was just illustrating the many issues I still had to think through.

Brainstorm: When to Ask a Dumb Question

When do you ask a dumb question? How do you balance the desire to impress your mentors and business acquaintances but also learn from them when you're confused?

On the one hand, honesty should rule. If you're meeting a venture capitalist and don't understand a term she uses, ask. It's an educational experience. If your business is really struggling, tell your advisors and get advice.

On the other hand, like it or not, you always need to spin. What if you need that VC to fund you? If you come across like a total ignoramus it won't help your chances. If you're young, people will understand a certain amount of not-knowing but still expect a baseline of knowledge and expertise.

Even now, I am sometimes in meetings when someone introduces a foreign concept. Should I ask for an explanation or go with the flow? In some instances I am supposed to be the expert and to show uncertainty would damage my credibility. So I take a note to look up the concept online or—better yet—ask someone "offline," after the meeting.

Particularly for green entrepreneurs, managing your relationship with experienced businesspeople and all their varied expectations takes some practice. In general it is best to ask the dumb question, even though you don't want to turn every moment into a teaching one. Focus on the *right* time to ask a question—it might not be when the question crosses your mind, but it still should be asked eventually.

"How is all this sounding to you, Ben?" Mike asked. The room went silent. The only noise was my brain chewing on Greg's questions.

"Wow, really helpful," I ventured. "I guess I'm unsure where I go from here. At a general level, it seems the idea may have a future, but differentiating it from competition is going to be key. I also need to better understand the budgets and numbers of smaller governments to determine the 'market size' more."

"Right, Ben," Greg responded. "There's a lot to work through. The hardest part of your work is done: discovering a need in the market and coming up with an early prototype to solve that. Now you need to further prove that the need is one your customers will pay money for."

"How do we do that? A lot of cities have told me they're interested in something like this, but talk is much different than writing a check," I said.

"Yes. And many prospects may not want to buy until others are using the product," Greg said.

"So you think we should go beta?" Mike asked Greg, half-knowing the answer.

Greg nodded. I narrowed my eyes and raised my eyebrows to signal confusion.

"I think you should go find a few beta testers who will use the prototype and give you feedback and endorsements. You'll need to find innovative kinds of cities, but if you can sign them up by not charging anything, it'll really help your b-plan's credibility."

"I'm not sure a city would start using a product when Ben's not available to explain and support it. . . . After all, he does go back to school soon. Do we need to hire someone to work with the beta testers while Ben's in school?" Dad asked.

"Yes, but it needn't be a full-time person. There are firms that provide tech support for software companies; maybe one of them could do it at a discount rate. Let me talk to some friends and see if we can't find someone to help out here. In the meantime, you should interview some local programmers and see if they could work part-time to answer a call that comes during the day," Greg said.

Two clear action items: find beta testers, find tech support. Mike smiled at me, which I took as my cue.

"Well, thanks a lot, Greg, this has been amazingly helpful, really appreciate your time."

"It was my pleasure, Ben. You've got something going here. Ben, as you embark on this journey, most people are going to tell you to give up, to just be normal, to quit being a dreamer. I want you to never listen to any of them and keep pounding away at your vision. Good things come from the desire to make them happen."

It was a moving message. Like all inspirational messages, the timing made the difference: it squelched any self-doubts that arose during the meeting. And it was from someone who cared, someone who was looking me in the eye (as opposed to a bland poster smile). The line rings true to this day. For the first time, after meeting Greg, I thought that Comcate could be more than just an idea.

>>

As the first successful businessperson I met, Greg became my model. I wanted to read the magazines Greg read. I wanted to read his books. I wanted to figure out who else he met with. I wanted to know who his friends were. I wanted to know how he thought and how he formed opinions, so I could shape them and digest them. I continued my aggressive path of self-learning if for no other reason than to better understand the man who was Greg Prow.

Brain Trust: Taking Mentor Relationships to the Next Level

BY BRAD FELD

My first mentor was my Dad. I remember going for a long walk with him near our house in Dallas when I was thirteen, when he actively stepped out of "Dad" mode and went into "business mentor mode" for the first time. Part of the brilliance of his mentoring was that he realized I needed nonparental mentors too, so he introduced me to a patient of his, Gene Scott, who had been an executive at several computer companies in the 1960s and 1970s. As a teenager, I had a monthly dinner with "Mr. Scott" and I got my first taste of how rewarding a mentoring relationship can be.

In college, I started two companies that both failed, but my mentors (and my Dad) stayed close to me and helped me learn, struggle through the businesses, and accept failure.

In my first successful company, Feld Technologies, one of our early clients—Stewart Forbes—became another influential mentor. Stewart taught me how to learn by actively working with my mentors, rather than just observing them. I learned that an active mentoring relationship—regular communications, a two-way exchange of ideas, and even some disagreement—is much more effective than a "lecture-style" relationship.

When I was in my early twenties, my uncle Charlie Feld entered the scene. Charlie was the CIO at Frito-Lay and one of the most respected CIOs in industry. Whenever Charlie was in Boston, he invited me along, unashamed to have his nephew in tow. He taught me to always be being willing to include younger people in your activities so they can learn. And with his help, I learned a lot.

Not all my mentors were businesspeople. Eric von Hippel, my graduate advisor at MIT, pushed me to figure out deeper lessons about life. When I dropped out of a Ph.D. program, got divorced, and sold my first company—all in the same year—Eric was there for me day and night to help me work through my first major personal crisis and determine how I wanted to respond to it. Eric taught me how to discover what I really wanted to do with my life, and then spend all my time doing it. Without a mentor, it would have taken me a much longer time to answer this critical question. Eric may have been in academia, but he could still play "life coach" to me, a good reminder that sometimes the best mentors guide you in areas outside their official domain of expertise.

When I sold my first company at age twenty-seven, I gained two great mentors—Len Fassler and Jerry Poch. In addition to giving me solid business advice, Len taught me how to be gracious in every situation. He also emphasized the value of sticking with something to the very end, whether good or bad. Jerry taught me how to always be direct and clear, no matter what the news. Even if I hadn't gotten a dime for my first company, Len and Jerry's lessons about graciousness, persistence, and candor would have more than paid for themselves many times over.

When I look back on these and all the other mentors I've had (and continue to have today) and the people whom I now mentor, one thing stands out: the rare but brilliant moment when the relationship shifts, the distinction between mentor and mentee dissolves, and you become "co-mentors." Even if you aren't peers, the learning becomes bidirectional. Everyone in a mentoring relationship should strive for this equilibrium, because it is here that the greatest learning occurs.

It's easy to take. It's harder to give. The value, and joy, you derive from a mentoring relationship corresponds with the effort you put into it. When there's a balance between the two the relationship can be extraordinary. Think about what you are learning from your mentors. Even more importantly, think about what you are teaching them.

Brad Feld is a venture capitalist based in Boulder, Colorado. He's a former entrepreneur, an avid marathoner, and active blogger at www.feld.com.

Signing Up Early Customers: Selling the Sizzle *and* the Steak

Everyone lives by selling something.
ROBERT LOUIS STEVENSON

Enough with focus groups. I wanted customers!

I called Ramsey in Antioch and told him I thought the product was ready for a more serious look. Our product prototype, based on his original comments, had come a long way. There were three sections in the product eFeedbackManager (eFM): a citizen panel, where residents could submit their gripes online; an employee panel, where city employees could respond to and resolve requests; and an administrative panel, where a secretary could customize the system, run reports, and so on. Looking back, it was probably version .001, but it worked. Ramsey agreed to the meeting and invited me back to do a pitch to his staff.

I brought my Dad and Mike Patterson along as well to offer credibility. Ramsey was bound to have some concerns. Is Comcate legit, or is it just Ben having a good time? Mike Patterson, given his involvement in Silicon Valley, would be able to offer the necessary assurances . . . even if some of them were hovering in the future tense. A good way to boost credibility is to have other people endorse your work and dependability.

>>

I remember standing in the parking lot outside Antioch City Hall with Dad and Mike. I was shaking with nervousness. Not sorta nervous. Nervous of the teeth-chattering, knees unsteady, throat tight sort. When consumed by anxiety even the smallest tasks seem beyond manageable. For one, I spent precious minutes trying to figure out where to keep my business cards since my suit jacket pockets were still sewn shut.

Over and over in my head I visualized shaking hands with Ramsey, smiling, and saying "Hey there, how are you?" For some reason I could never get past that moment—just that initial handshake, over and over.

"Ben, how you doin' over there?" Mike asked, as he slipped on his jacket.

"Fine," I lied.

"Good. Believe in yourself. And the product. You'll do great."

It's amazing how such simple positive reinforcement can have such a meaningful impact.

The nervousness proved to be like cotton candy—it melted upon contact in a handshake. The handshake, and the meeting for that matter, felt like it lasted a minute. There were a total of nine people in the room, the largest crowd to whom I had ever presented. With all eyes on me during the pitch, I felt a power unlike any other. The room was at my beck and call—except for that finance guy snoozing in the back. I smoothly transitioned from one idea to the next and answered each question. And from that meeting on, each time I was put at the front, I knew I was capable of hitting a home run.

>>

After the department heads left, we sat around with Ramsey, the decision maker, to discuss next steps. "We'll be a beta," he said finally. Everything before those words sounded like pig Latin. *Yes!* It was unbelievable. We were shocked. We were expecting him to talk it over with his department heads before committing to the program as a citywide tool to manage requests. But hey—he just said it—they were going to be a beta tester.

If only *saying* it meant *doing* it. . . .

When we left the building after the meeting, Dad and Mike both told me what a good job I'd done. I was really pumped and proud. For the first time it felt like all my efforts had been vindicated. Plus, it gave me a great talking point for the meeting the following night with the business bigwigs (and potential investors down the road) who Mike had invited to dinner. I arrived home late at night and visited the City of Antioch website again, reading each page in awestruck detail. I couldn't believe it—a real city was going to pay Comcate, eventually, for this little product of mine.

>>

The next night my routine felt familiar: tan suit, play hooky from P.E., and head to Silicon Valley. Dad, Mike, and I drove to a Chinese restaurant where Mike had assembled a cadre of business friends. There were five guests: Greg Lahann, a partner at Novus Ventures; Tim Conley, CFO of public company Tumbleweed; Carol Rutlen, CEO of a start-up software company; Betty Jo Charles, a partner at PricewaterhouseCoopers who worked with start-ups; and Geoff Darby, a local, wealthy "mentor capitalist." Some of the dinner guests were already sitting at the table when I arrived and they eyed me up and down, unsure whether to be impressed by my height, as I headed to the bathroom. After a pit stop that necessitated wiggling and rewiggling my tie to make sure it was as good as it could be, I sat down at our table. Everyone offered introductions: "I manage a fund of about $250 million." "I manage all the financial operations for a company traded on NASDAQ." "I run a successful software company." Fortunately, Mike had gathered "smart money"—folks with cash who also had brains.

I instantly felt a different dynamic than during the Antioch meeting the evening before. These were people who were quicker on their feet, more energized, and ready to encourage me *and* nurse their own egos at the same time. Being new to the game, I wasn't able to customize my presentation based on this new kind of audience, but over time the skill of off-the-cuff adaptation was one I employed effectively.

At a tactical level, the folks at the dinner affirmed the worthiness of trying to sign up beta testers. They also encouraged me to find an interim CEO who could help sign and implement beta clients and shore up the business plan to raise angel financing.

Brainstorm: Asking Questions:
There's a Right and a Wrong Way

In the early goings of any new endeavor you will want to ask questions of people who have been there and done that. It's not easy. But asking good questions is at the heart of business— from sales pitches to hiring people to merely clarifying what needs to be done and by what date.

The most difficult questions to ask are those that intend to elicit a response beyond yes or no—what are known as *open* questions. Say you want to find out what's on a prospect's mind. What is that individual's *real* concerns? The best approach is to probe on value judgments. "It's been a real difficult time, recently . . . ," someone tells you. Your response could be, "What do you mean, difficult? Can you be specific?" Questions that start with "How" are also likely to elicit wide-ranging and helpful responses.

Then there's the content of the question itself. Good, original questions are hard to come by. That's why you'll find the most impressive person in the boardroom asking the best questions. I take notice when someone asks me, "How did running a business affect your relationship with your friends and parents?" as opposed to, "How did you balance it all?" The first question is richer and should be more provocative. It will answer the second question but with flavor and depth.

Before asking a question remember who you're meeting with. When I meet with senior business executives who have been asked the same questions over and over by the press, I resolve not to be "just another peanut in the gallery." I try to ask thoughtful questions and focus, when appropriate, on nonbusiness issues. Once I met with a very high-profile CEO—we'll call him John. I wanted to talk to John about Comcate and business but I could tell he wasn't interested in that. He saw our meeting as a way to get away from the daily grind of running a high-powered company. So I took a different tack, and asked him, point blank, if he believed in

(Continued)

God. While religion (and politics) are generally thought to be taboo in business conversation, many people (though not all) find it a refreshing change. How someone thinks about nonprofessional issues can also give me a different kind of insight into his thought process. John and I had a wonderful one-hour conversation, me probing, he responding and elaborating. As we walked out of the café together, John said, "You know, I really enjoyed our conversation. And by the way, you should meet the second-in-charge here, his name's Richard. He'll be a great guy to know for your business." I followed up, and Richard proved invaluable in providing connections and advice for Comcate.

Like most meetings of this sort there wasn't any golden specific advice but rather just lots of encouragement—which is helpful!

Once again, only in hindsight do I realize how lucky I was to have such an experienced group of folks at the dinner table. Yet, they were there because I had pursued a relationship with Mike Patterson. I could have let it simmer out after our initial meeting, but I kept in touch, and it paid off. Luck introduced me to Mike; hard work introduced me to his friends.

>>

The news kept getting better. During spring of my eighth-grade year I scheduled some meetings with city managers in Southern California via referrals from a partner at Dad's law firm. Mom has always reluctantly called me in sick at school (I helped her think of different kinds of doctors) when I had to attend meetings, relieving me of "excused absence" procedures. For the first time, Dad wouldn't join me on the trip because he had other commitments. This didn't faze me. My sales pitch was coming along. I kept revising it based on feedback from Dad ("Slow down, *slow* down") and from my readings on presentation style and techniques. I would practice in front of the mirror, tape myself with the videocamera, and go through it screen by screen on my own computer. I practiced over and over again, which contributed to a high degree of confidence during the real thing.

Brainstorm: I Have a Strategic Plan.
It's Called Doing Things.

Good businesspeople obsess over the pragmatic outcome of their actions. They are constantly making decisions and evaluating the results.

Southwest Airlines, one of the most successful businesses of our day, has a smart CEO. Herb Kelleher once responded to an interviewer: "We have a strategic plan. It's called doing things." Similarly, according to business lore, the successful American financier J. P. Morgan once paid $25,000 for a piece of paper that contained the ultimate secret to success: each day write down the things that need to be done, and do them.

In the early days of any new business, it's easier to plan than to act. It's easier to strategize than to actually *do stuff*.

Whether during my early successes signing up clients or in my upcoming failures, through and through I tried to keep action as the centerpiece of my strategy. I learned much more by obsessing over the results of different approaches than I did theorizing how a certain action *could* end up.

Think who, what, when, why, how. The answer to "when" is *now*, the answer to "who" is *you*, and the only other questions that matter are "what" and "how."

Since I was too young to rent a car, Mom came with me to do the driving. She never came inside to the meetings; rather, she checked out local parks, waited in the car, read books. Besides driving, she often let me reflect on a meeting (which clarified and engrained my thinking about a particular prospect), encouraged me to write down notes, and navigated the sprawling highways of Southern California with prowess.

The first meeting was with the City of Burgon Hills.[1] Burgon Hills is a media capital in Southern California. It's a full-service,

---

1 Names of all individuals related to Burgon Hills, and the city name, have been changed.

complex city that provides police, fire, power, sewage, water, and all the other standard big-city services. Their city manager at the time—Bud Roberts—was well-known and highly regarded by his peers. I had thought I was meeting only with Bud, but in fact he'd invited a crew of city staff and assistants. Right off the bat, Bud fell in love with the product, and with me. He totally dug the idea of streamlining government with better technology. With the tone set from the top, no one else in the room raised objections. (A strong CEO!) I thrived on his enthusiasm and displayed my A game.

"So what do you want of us?" Bud asked when I was finished answering questions. I had never heard that question before— usually I have to proactively ask.

"Well," I answered. "I want feedback, which you've already given me. I want Burgon Hills to be the Southern California leader of this product and join Antioch in Northern California. And third, I would be grateful for introductions to other managers." (I always asked for these three things: feedback, a contract, and referrals.)

Bud verbally committed in the meeting that Burgon Hills would be our charter user in SoCal *and* he would introduce me to other managers. He asked an assistant to the city manager—Rita— to work with me to get the project moving. I was stunned. Plus, over the next few months, Bud sent out emails to more than fifteen managers, single-handedly making deals happen for Comcate and me. He turned out to be one of my biggest supporters. When I arrived at my afternoon meeting at a neighboring city that day, the city manager mentioned that Bud had already sent him an email saying I was the most impressive fourteen-year-old he'd ever met. When I got home from SoCal, I had an email from Rita asking for a contract. I closed my bedroom door gently, and blasted Van Halen's song "Jump" as loud as I could from my computer.

>>

It had been an amazing few months. Dad always says it was Burgon Hills—a city with which we had no personal "insider" deal at all, and a city I visited on my own—that woke him up to an exhilarating yet scary reality: this thing was the real deal. No more screwing around. We now had fiduciary obligations to a real, large local government. We also realized how potent the "kid factor" was, and that my age could be a resource. But these few months are also a great example of how quickly fortunes can turn in a start-up. I never would have guessed that neither Antioch nor Burgon Hills would go on to become committed, paying clients. I never would have guessed that our relationship in Burgon Hills would turn to shambles and become one of our biggest headaches. I never would have guessed that our champions in both cities would depart before we would go live with our service. But for now, I was on my high horse. Things were happening, and summer was not long off.

Confronting Failure . . . and Bouncing Back

Success consists of going from failure to failure without loss of enthusiasm.
WINSTON CHURCHILL

I graduated from middle school in June 2002 and delivered the commencement address after being chosen by my classmates. My message embodied the worldview I had adopted in my entrepreneurship: think differently, change the world. I recited the Apple "Think Different" advertising campaign. I recited an anonymous poem about youthful optimism:

> For I am young, and young people always believe that tomorrow will be better than today. Youth try the impossible. Scale the mountain that is supposed to be inaccessible. And dare the things that age will fear.

The next morning, I was pitching Comcate to potential customers, but things had changed. It was a totally different environment, one where I couldn't coast and relax. I couldn't just let words fly out of my mouth and sound articulate, an autopilot mode that had worked in school. I needed to plan, think, and focus on matching the intellectual and rhetorical abilities of the adults in the meetings. Even more, I needed to influence what they were thinking in order to sell them something. This required a level of focus well above that employed during my graduation speech, and as such, it was a greater thrill, even though the audience was three and not three hundred.

>>

We had two cities onboard—Antioch and Burgon Hills—and figuring out how people were actually going to use the product was in many ways a thornier challenge than selling it in the first place. Anytime a new program touches a lot of people across an organization you encounter varying levels of flak, regardless of the initiative's merits, because resistance to change is among our most reflexive defense mechanisms. I would soon learn that a signed contract does not automatically mean a happy client. A happy client means all the users are trained on the application and reaping the promised benefits.

>>

Any first-time salesman can attest to the deep angst associated with selling someone something when you're not sure how it will *really* work out. We promise, promise, promise, but until we have real case studies of successful use, our solution is unproven—and that's nerve-racking.

Mike Ramsey, bogged down in another project, was not being responsive in Antioch; Burgon Hills was, so they received my attention. I never had a customer before, let alone implemented a software product in one of California's most complex local governments. With little leadership from my end, the process became a slow-motion train wreck. I had no original ideas on how to deal with the city's "legacy" data and how to account for it in the new system. I provided no proactive suggestions for overcoming basic customization obstacles. At one point I told Rita that I had never done this before so "thanks in advance for your patience." Can you imagine a vendor saying that to you? She graciously responded, "Neither have I." Honesty created a new bond!

>>

The summer of 2002 gave me the first taste of life as a "real" road warrior. I spent about a day a week in Southern California. I would drag my ass out of bed at some early hour, get a ride to Oakland Airport, and board a Southwest plane to Los Angeles International Airport. If I went by myself and only to Burgon Hills, I would hail a cab to City Hall, spend the day there, grab lunch with the clients or visit my favorite Ben's Café (where I ordered an avocado salad and ice water), then fly home in the evening. I started recognizing certain people who always took the 5:10 P.M. commuter flight home, and even figured out how to be super-efficient on the phone with Southwest ("I'd like to modify an existing itinerary" gets you farther faster than "I wanna change my flight").

After several trips, Burgon Hills proposed to pay for all my expenses. The licensing agreement was still held up in the city attorney's office, so we hadn't been paid our $7,000 beta contract fee yet. Covering my expenses was a reasonable offer but it took me aback. Since I would be doing extended consulting to get the project going, I had to come up with an hourly billing rate! I chose $30 an hour, added all my travel expenses, subtracted a few bucks here and there for "investment in client relationship," and then sent them Comcate Invoice #001. I don't know what they thought when they saw the number 001 on the invoice but I'm glad I was truthful because every time I look at the framed check for $429 on my wall I know that it really was the first. And every time I see the framed check for $40,000 next to it, I'm reminded of how fast Comcate grew. . . .

>>

Burgon Hills also was home to a generational battle. Here I was, the fourteen-year-old software vendor with marching orders from the fifty-six-year-old city manager to implement a software product. Standing in the way was the sixty-something city outreach director—let's call him Jack—a former Rotary Club president, military hero, and beloved city employee who personally handled many of the complaints routed through City Hall. Jack had his own way of doing things and he'd done them for years with good ole-fashioned paper and pencil. He even bragged about keeping his pager on all night in case a Burgon Hills citizen had an issue and wanted to get in touch with someone right away. Yet Bud, the city manager, wanted Jack's office to be modernized so everyone else in the organization could gain visibility on what Jack was doing—and I was charged with accomplishing this task. But Jack was stiff. He simply didn't want to change, he didn't see the point, and he was only open to talking about it because Bud wanted him to.

A lifelong resident of Burgon Hills, Jack sported a dark, unruly mustache that rattled me a little bit. The battle with Jack was extreme but representative of early pushback I received during my presentations to sales prospects. Older folks saw technology as something only young people could use. Had I been a fifty-year-old salesperson saying "Hey, even I can use this thing!" it surely would have been an easier sell.

"I will respect what you're doing here, I just don't want to use it. Paper, pencil—always works, always used it," he said in our first of several difficult one-on-one meetings.

"The problem, Jack, is that you represent a large percentage of the service requests directed through City Hall. If your stuff isn't tracked in the system, the citywide data become much less valuable," I answered.

He didn't say anything.

"The city manager's office wants visibility across the whole city, including *your* information," I added. Boss mandate was the best card I could play.

"Look, Bud wants this to happen, so I'll support it. Just not for my stuff," he said.

"Is it the computer? You don't want to use your computer? You'd rather use paper?"

"Yeah, it just doesn't work as well for me. I have a great system in place and don't plan on changing it."

"What if someone else entered the information for you?"

"What, like a secretary?"

"Yeah."

"Maybe that could work, if you found a good secretary."

We could figure something out, I thought, not quite believing myself. I thanked Jack for his time and went to the next meeting.

>>

I was never told why Bud asked me to persuade Jack to become computer-literate. Had others tried and failed? Was Bud, a mentor to me in one sense, trying to teach a lesson involving cross-generational advocacy? Or was the point for me to simply self-teach the technique of conversing with a client who, under all reasonable circumstances, wasn't interested in using technology to improve the ease and efficiency of performing his job? I was never able to "connect" with Jack, and we ultimately went our separate ways. I only hoped that, maybe, some small nugget bearing technology's potential had been lodged in his brain. . . .

>>

As the summer's end grew near, I started getting frustrated. Endless hours in Burgon Hills were leading nowhere—the city was simply too big, with too many employees trying to derail the project.[1] One woman wanted us to build her a custom application to track youth employment applications. Another wanted to integrate her tree-tracking application with our product. There seemed to be a lot of individuals fighting for what would suit them personally.

Outside of Burgon Hills, I was conducting at least a couple of Web demos or in-person pitches a week to new cities with little success. Despite the momentum I gained from a lunch with a quasi-retired local government legend, Tom Lewcock of Sunnyvale, who would go on to become one of Comcate's most vital supporters, his referrals were dragging out.[2] People were supportive, I was getting face time, but they wouldn't bite. I credit this equally to a product that wasn't quite up to snuff, B-grade presentations on my end, and an incomplete sales methodology that overlooked proper follow-up and materials.

>>

Our competitors—well-established companies and fledgling start-ups like ourselves—were turning up the heat, too. Negative ads.

---

1 Later I would learn the true meaning of "buy-in" and discover its significance in all new organization-wide projects.

2 We also asked Tom to be an interim CEO, even though he had no business experience. We were shocked that he gave our offer serious consideration, but he ultimately came back and said no. But, after making a "big ask" you improve your chances at getting a "little ask". Our "little ask" was his joining our advisory board, which I was forming at the time.

Brainstorm: Building Resilience—
A Transferable Quotient

How well do you weather hardships? Your answer may be what sets you apart. We all go through rough times. The most successful people don't just survive, they thrive.

I believe resilience is a skill that can be acquired. It's all about the little things. You build resilience by finishing small goals you set even if you feel like quitting. One thing I focus on, for example, is time on the treadmill. Say I'm going to be on the treadmill for thirty minutes, and twenty-three minutes into it I feel like quitting. If I stay on, and fight through the pain screaming from my feet and/or quads, I have contributed a bit to my resilience quotient (RQ).

My RQ can be applied throughout my life—being resilient in one setting will help me be resilient in unrelated others. As the COO search raged on, in my workouts I stayed on the treadmill the entire time. I studied for the full hour during a study hall. I drove through a rainstorm, did a demo of my product, drove home, and did the necessary follow-up, all while nursing a stomachache. I wanted to get the job done and endure an uncomfortable day. Because I knew that grappling with all that life throws at me on a day-to-day basis would help me be resilient in the face of a traumatic and extraordinary situation, such as hiring an executive to run my company.

If I can get up today, I can get up any day.

During the perfect storm, you must have a high resilience quotient. Prepare for it.

Overhyped sales literature. There were numerous tools of the "attack" trade. I lost a lucrative deal to another company despite the inordinate time and energy I invested courting the city. When I later heard our competitors were talking to yet another one of "my" cities, I exchanged emails with Dad, stealing a line from *Marketing High Technology,* by William Davidow:

Dad,

E-government marketing is civilized warfare. If we
find that metaphor too brutal, we shouldn't enlist.
As long as aggressive competitors exist we will be
under attack. Our competitor's job is to capture
business and then defend that new perimeter. So
is ours.

Every entrepreneur can sympathize: you're feeling invincible
after a rash of deals, press, and leads, and a few months later you
feel defeated and cheated of successes that they—the ubiquitous
"they" who we see as the chief causes of our own misfortunes—said
were done deals. I remember talking on the phone with Mike Patterson on a foggy afternoon one day in August as I described to
him the different leads I was tracking in Excel.

"Antioch's gone dormant, Burgon Hills's being derailed, none
of my central California leads are returning calls, San Ricardo just
bought GovStrategy. . . ."

Silence. Mike knew what I was waiting for, and he didn't give it
to me.

"So Ben, what are you going to do about it? What are the next
steps? Where are the bright spots?"

He delivered these words so naturally I just considered it an
ordinary response, and my mentor's outlook translated into an
unquestioned habit of mine: be persistent. Little did I know this
and other habits I formed during the early days of Comcate would
continue to pay dividends to this day in everything I do. I was so
lucky with the advisors I had—none of them wanted to give up,
none of them would let me give up.

>>

During this rough stretch I would occasionally ask myself the questions that lurk in the minds of so many entrepreneurs: "Funda-
mentally, is it worth it?" The 4 A.M. alarm clocks for a flight to L.A.,
missing a crucial basketball workout, spending a little less time with
personal friends. The same work-life balance issues that bedevil
adults trying to juggle a marriage, kids, and a company affected
me, too, though mine centered around my occasional absences
from "conventional" childhood activities. I remember a prominent

Silicon Valley venture capitalist once telling me he thought I was too invested in my Comcate world and that "I had my whole life to start companies." He may have had a point at the time, as I struggled through this period. I'm just glad I didn't follow his advice, because then the story would stop here.

My whole life I've wanted to be held to the same standard as any entrepreneur, not a kid-entrepreneur. If I gave up, people would forgive me: he's just a kid, they would say. If I were a thirty-year-old entrepreneur and gave up, people would say instead, "He has no balls." Since I held myself to the latter standard, I didn't want to be accused of having no balls. It's a slog, my advisors said; dig in and make stuff happen.

>>

"Dig in" meant, for me, "Do what it takes" to help the business. And this meant give lots of face time to people who could help Comcate overcome its woes.

Once, a couple years later, I trekked to El Dorado County in California, about a three-hour drive northeast from San Francisco—a good example of my commitment to face time. I had come to enjoy these frequent car journeys, each small town home to some newspaper or diner that can lift any tired traveler's weary spirits.

After three hours in the car, one hour getting lost, and one hour in my target meeting, I turned around to make the three-and-a-half-hour journey home (three hours plus a half hour getting lost). I made my way to the Highway 50 west corridor, which would take me a good forty miles. Ah, a long stretch of California highway. I cruised up to 80 mph and rolled down the window. The radio that should have spit out "California Dreamin'" by The Mamas and The Papas instead gave only static.

Within twenty minutes I arrived back in radio-signal zone and figured my BlackBerry would reconnect, too. But to confirm my suspicion, I would have to first find it. With my left hand steering to keep me in the left lane, I leaned on my right buttock and with my right arm reached into my bag placed on the floor under the passenger's seat. *Where is it?* I didn't immediately find it with my hand. To give sight to my lost hand I darted my eyes down once to see if I could locate my BlackBerry in the bag next to me.

By the time I blinked my eyes back to the road, it was too late.

My car swerved just a little to the left, hit a groove, and in only mild panic, I compensated by turning the wheel back right. By now both hands were stationed firmly on the steering wheel. A car in the right lane whizzed by me, and afraid I overcompensated, as they always warn you in driver school, I turned the steering wheel back to the left, hoping to realign in the center of my lane. But in that readjustment I hit yet another groove, this one big, a sign of the old highway on which I rode, and it rattled the car. I compensated right, then left, then right again to meet a slight curve in the road. My speed crept to 85 mph until I realized I was traveling way too fast. I slammed on the brakes, continued to swerve, and then around the next curve my car began spinning. One moment I swayed like a hammock in the wind and the next moment I was controlling maniacal helicopter wings. I did three 360s on the ground, and spun out of my lane farther left into the center divide. Forty feet of grass and shrubs separated the westbound traffic from the busy eastbound traffic. As my car spun— me gripping the wheel strongly and slamming on the brakes—I was certain I would die. This wasn't exactly the kind of face time I planned on. I wanted face time with Comcate supporters, not with the face of the Grim Reaper.

So this is it, I thought. *Now I'm going to die. At least I lived happily and did my thing.* Those words immediately came to mind as my car spun, a dummy driver watching his all-too-short life being snatched away because of a reflexive urge to check his BlackBerry while driving.

As my car screeched into the center divide, I prayed it would stop moving so I wouldn't hit oncoming traffic. I closed my eyes, my foot pressed still harder to the brake pedal. I started coughing. Dust and weeds coupled with the bitter aroma of fear and guilt produced dirtied air I didn't want to breathe. The car stopped. I broke down, sobbing. My tears weren't heroic but defeated. I looked at myself with a kind of scorn reserved for consequences brought onto yourself. I was helpless, sweating compulsively, shaking, trying to comprehend a near-death experience.

And then, the BlackBerry email/phone that had caused the distraction that led to my accident rang. So it *was* in my bag, after all. *Should I even pick it up? What does one do in this situation? I'm sit-*

ting in the middle of a center divide in a freeway with my car probably majorly messed up. Do I answer the phone? Sensibly, I didn't pick it up. Instead, I drove the car off the highway at the next exit to examine the damage. While stopped I checked my voicemail and my emotions did their own 180: a city prospect wanted a follow-up demonstration. . . . Tomorrow! Nice!

The next day, en route to the meeting, the right front tire, which, unbeknownst to me, had been damaged in my off-road excursion, flew off my car while I was driving down the center lane of Highway 101. A police escort stopped all traffic on this major California artery, took me off the road, and called a tow truck. I never made it to the pitch.

>>

Failures, obstacles, even car crashes are all part of the start-up experience. Ups and downs are the definitive indication that you are doing something entrepreneurial. If your record is spotless, then you haven't been an entrepreneur. If the only mistakes you've made are on school papers or in mishandling a report in a big corporation, those aren't spots. It's the spots from the school of hard knocks that matter. They matter because how you confront real failure is right up there with self-confidence, drive, and luck as a critical ingredient for success.

When you are controlling your own destiny, as most entrepreneurs are, it is easy to place all the blame on yourself. Don't. Circumstances matter and not all circumstances are within your control. For failure due to circumstances out of your control, try to learn from it and then embrace the mantra, "Shit happens." Instead, figure out what you *can* control and constantly reinvent it. If it ain't broke, fix it anyway, because you won't know when it's broke to begin with—so preempt failure caused by complacency.

I also looked at all my failures that summer with a sense of urgency. I needed more successes. I was about to start high school and my business needed help. Fast.

Brainstorm: How to Create and Leverage an Advisory Board

An advisory board is an informal version of a board of directors since it's not legally affiliated with your company and it provides advice, not mandates. Advisory boards can be critical to entrepreneurs short on resources, guidance, or both. Usually an advisory board means *free* advice.

Forming an advisory board isn't as hard as it sounds. Start by listing your goals. What *kind* of advice do you need? Are you just looking for credibility? What type of commitment will you require from your advisory board members? A meeting every quarter? A conference call each month? Then, come up with your dream team list, work within your network, and reach out to people you respect.

I needed advice on how to start a business and advice on how to sell into the local government market. I worked within my small network to find people who could help. I spread the word—I was looking for advisors who knew local government, who knew how to develop software, or who knew how to develop an efficient marketing function. Our initial advisory board comprised two retired city managers, a CEO of a software start-up, a quasi-retired technology executive and lawyer, and a financial executive/VC. Securing a few quality people early helps—people join advisory boards, in part, for networking opportunities.

Keep in mind, though, that sometimes the best advisory boards offer credibility more than advice. That's why your advisory board should be a blend of big names with no time, and no names with plenty of time. The big names should be industry titans who can be useful in the sales process.

We scheduled meetings at least two or three times a year with occasional conference calls, too. What kinds of issues do you discuss during these meetings? Here are some topics discussed at Comcate's advisory board meetings:

- *Product road map.* Where will the product be going in the next two to three years and how can we ensure the vision is consistent with customer needs?

- *Recruitment.* What are the ideal qualities of the new XYZ employee? Does anyone have good candidate leads?
- *Competitive landscape.* Is the market seeing new entrants? What kinds of success has our competition had? How can we differentiate ourselves?
- *Financials and cash management.* How efficiently are we managing cash flow?

Finally, even if you don't run a company, consider forming a "personal board of advisors" who can commit to helping you in your career.

Go ahead—ask someone to join your advisory board. You may be surprised at how many people will feel flattered that you want to value their advice on a regular basis, and then say yes.

Hiring an Interim CEO: My First Big Mistake

The only real mistake is the one from which we learn nothing.
JOHN POWELL, WESTERN FRONTIERSMAN

The bus only moves if the right person is driving it. As I learned, sometimes it's better to have no driver at all than somebody who will take you backwards.

>>

I had been admitted to a rigorous high school in San Francisco, and as the fall of 2002 loomed, I knew that with our beta clients up and running Comcate couldn't be put on hold while I tended to my studies. Dad, Mike Patterson, and I agreed that we should try to find a three-month interim CEO to help write a business plan to grow the company and determine its long-term viability.

A mutual friend introduced us to Andy Snow, the ex-CEO of an internet company who was looking for work. His background and availability seemed almost too good to be true.[1]

>>

During the dot-com boom Andy ran an online sporting goods marketplace, raised three rounds of VC funding, and grew his com-

---

1 The name of this person has been changed.

pany to several hundred employees. His picture was even on the front page of the *Wall Street Journal* after closing a key deal! If there was any better candidate for an interim position, we couldn't imagine who it would be. We invited Andy to our house one summer evening to talk about Comcate.

We asked Andy about his prior company, which had imploded in the dot-com burst. He went on. And on. And on. He used buzzwords like "leverage," "boil-the-ocean," and "business processes." We should have seen this as a warning sign—he simply hadn't let go of his old company, for one, and two, he seemed long on platitude and short on substance. This being said, he did possess some important entrepreneurial experiences and seemed charismatic.

After Andy left, we had our customary postmortem standing meeting in our dining room, since meetings are always more efficient when done standing.

"Well, whaddya think?" I asked Mike. Dad and I were always anxious to hear Mike's thoughts.

"Ben, you heard what I heard. He can't get over that last company. And hey—I don't blame him. Tough ending. But I wonder whether he's past that and could focus on *Comcate*," Mike said.

"But who else do we have? Ben's going back to school in a few weeks and it doesn't look like we have anyone else, right?" Dad said.

"That's true. And he's certainly got the start-up/VC experience and could help on the b-plan. I think we keep moving forward with Andy but continue to probe other candidates. We've gotten a little unlucky with the other interim guys Greg Lahann introduced us to—none is available. Ben, follow up with that other guy Prow introduced you to. Let's see what we get there," Mike said.

>>

That conversation and many others like it took place in our modest San Francisco home. Contrary to the typical media fantasy of yacht-cruising millionaires wheeling and dealing their way to the next big technology fortune, most entrepreneurship happens in quite ordinary circumstances. Dorm rooms, garages, kitchens, cafés . . . even bedrooms. Ordinary people, ordinary circumstances, ordinary conversations. But unusual passion.

>>

Despite the early-warning signs, we met with Andy a second time. Andy announced he was comfortable working in one of three capacities: (a) as a consultant to write a good business plan, (b) as a full-time CEO until the company raised money, or (c) as a full-time interim CEO for three months to continue to move the company forward. We decided that the last option made the most sense and agreed in principle that it would be great to work together. We only had to settle on a fair compensation package.

We worked late into the night to forge perhaps the most important agreement of my young company—Andy's job offer. However, the next morning marked my first day of high school, and freshman orientation beckoned. The Class of 2006 was going to a remote mountain setting to get to know each other for two days.

>>

As we drove across the Golden Gate Bridge, my new classmates sat around me on the bus. The bus typified high school life: people were assessing possible best friends and signaling out the losers, rap music screamed loudly from a boom box, the rowdy jocks had secured the seats at the back of the bus. I, on the other hand, sat aloof, and started sweating. My BlackBerry was losing signal! Andy was supposed to be emailing me his comp proposal any minute! Shit!

Upon my return, we hammered out a compensation package consisting of cash and housing. We let him stay in the in-law unit of our house for three months for free. Being in a "transitional" housing situation, this appealed to him. In hindsight, this housing accommodation was the stupidest thing we did—the unit literally shares a wall with my bedroom. Trust me: never mix personal and professional!

>>

I had high hopes for Andy, since he was the first credentialed, adult business partner I had worked with in my career. To help realize these high expectations, I tried to get him up to speed as quickly as possible. I inundated him with emails, reports, white papers, and other material on the market. He needed to acquire a basic level of understanding about the market, then learn how to do a demo, and then start work on the business plan.

Unfortunately, Andy's tenure at Comcate did not last. We did not see eye-to-eye on the little things. Or on the big things. There were communication breakdowns galore. I take part of the blame, seeing that—aside from my father—I had never worked intimately with another adult businessperson before. I didn't know how to relate. I made plenty of mistakes in my interactions with Andy. My style of giving feedback was as smooth as a bear gobbling up a fish from a stream—in-your-face and combative. I sometimes assumed the worst and didn't give him a fair shot. I bombarded him with emails about little things when I should have saved them for one round-up phone call or meeting.

I also learned another valuable lesson: a company should never hire a CEO who has too much personal "baggage"—distracting emotional events in his life that can reduce his focus on the company.

>>

With jobs scarce during the dot-com bust period, MBA students were probably inquiring at In-n-Out Burger for possible employment. So Andy, during his brief employment, easily found two competent business school students—one from U.C. Berkeley, the other from the University of San Francisco—each of whom devoted twenty hours a week for three months to Comcate . . . for free! (Who said never start a company in a recession?) They worked with and for Andy doing research centered around this question: Was Comcate's best chance as a small, cash-cow operation or could it scale to be a big company?

They delivered their final fifty-seven-page "white paper" three months later to the board of advisors. It had all the makings of a business plan and also listed various scenarios that tweaked geographic focus and friends and family investment. Their conclusion? Comcate could either be maintained as a small, family-run cash cow with no outside funding commitment, or if we wanted to grow it larger, we could hire an executive for $80K a year, link with distribution partners, and see if we could grow the company to be a national player. And then raise additional investment. In other words, if we stayed as a cottage industry company, operated by me

Brainstorm: Three Sure Ways to Maximize Luck

I made mistakes when we hired our interim CEO, but I also got unlucky. Sometimes that's the way things go. In my view, luck is the single most underrated component of success. Fortunately, there are many things you can do to maximize your chances of being lucky.

1. *Expose yourself to as much randomness as possible.* Attend conferences no one else is attending. Read books no one else is reading. Talk to people no one else is talking to. Who would have thought that giving a speech at a funeral at age twelve would introduce me to a man who would introduce me to my first business contact who would introduce me to several other important people in my life? That's luck. That's randomness.

2. *Trust in probabilities of luck.* I think life works in peaks and valleys. Every time luck doesn't go my way I believe a piece of good luck is right around the corner—you always bounce up after hitting rock bottom. Similarly, whenever I get lucky I prepare myself for weathering a dip. Knowing this, I can always mitigate a rough stretch and make the most of the good times.

3. *Trick yourself.* Self-deception is essential for high self-esteem. It's OK to take more credit than you deserve, in your own mind, for successes. It's OK to think that you can outwork and outpassion anyone who competes with you. It's OK to attribute soaring victories to a tireless work ethic. It's OK if these are slight exaggerations. After all, how many people attribute "good luck" to their wins? Far fewer than those who attribute "bad luck" to their losses! Stay humble, especially on the outside, but consider yourself (privately) as unstoppable.

and some advisors and consultants, we could expect slow, steady growth, but couldn't compete with bigger firms or get rich. Alternatively, and more aggressively, we could retain a "chief bottle washer"—or chief operating officer—to work full-time to grow the company and raise outside venture funding. (The title could have been CEO or president, but that would have meant a higher base salary.) This latter option was riskier but had a bigger upside.

>>

More risk, more upside. For entrepreneurs, it's a no-brainer: go for it.

Author Annie Dillard once said, "If we listened to our intellect, we'd never have a love affair. We'd never have a friendship. We'd never go into business, because we'd be too cynical. Well, that's nonsense. You've got to jump off cliffs all the time and build your wings on the way down."

We decided we wanted to jump off the cliff. We had to find a full-time COO who could help us build our wings.

The Hunt for a COO: Recruiting a Top Team

The guy. No special emphasis on either the *or* guy, *but no intervening pause, either. TheGuy. That's the person needed to head a start-up once it has grown beyond a seed. To wit, a stud, ideally, a big honkin' stud or a total fuckin' stud. He (or yes, she) will not lack for balls, at least in one sense, but in another will work his nuts off, or his ass off. A high-hustle guy. A total can-do guy. A winner. Smart. Someone with integrity off the charts. Scrappy. A kick-ass dude, a nail-eatin', nut-crushin' decision maker, a competitor with killer instincts. Someone who attracts and hires A's, unafraid to hire above himself. A player. A hitter.*

RANDALL STROSS, *eBoys*

The first hire in a start-up is the most important. Hire a B person and you probably will end up with a B company. The first hire in a start-up is also the most difficult for a founder. Will the person you hire nurture your baby or drop it over the ledge? Put you on the cover of *Business Week,* or push you out?

>>

We made a courageous decision and chose the riskier of the two paths presented to us in the interim CEO's research white paper. We still couched it as a contingency: *if* we couldn't find TheGuy (or TheGal) *then* we would remain a cottage industry. This made the process less scary. For some reason I doubted we'd find someone right to take over my baby—maybe because I was leading the executive search process. I had no experience or knowledge of this facet of business. That changed. Fast.

>>

Regardless of how smooth the process should run in *theory*, taking the leap—investing valuable resources to hire a total stranger who might have different ideas about where the company should go— is gut-wrenching and emotional.

It started easily. We first had to define the characteristics of the ideal chief cook and bottle washer. Mike Patterson, still my main mentor, gave me a sample executive job spec from a recruiter that I customized and sent around to my advisory board for feedback. Much of a job specification is boilerplate. I added a sentence to the candidate qualification section lifted from Jim Collins's *Good to Great*, "S/he will be able to translate the vision and broad strategic goals into concrete tactics and objectives. This individual will display compelling modesty, and be fanatically driven, infected with an incurable need to produce sustained results." Did that help narrow down the pool? Hardly. But it reminded us that we needed someone passionate about creating something and therefore willing to roll up his or her sleeves.

The friends and family investment pool allowed us to recruit a person who would be willing to start at a base salary of $90K plus stock options, bonuses, and commissions. While this kind of salary package would put its recipient far above most American wage earners, it is actually pretty darn low when you're talking about A-list CEOs. So we knew that we weren't going to get the next Jack Welch, Steve Jobs, or Meg Whitman.

Next, we had to spread the word as far and wide as possible. We posted the job opportunity on HotJobs.com and on the local universities' alumni job boards.

I received more than two hundred emails from serious people who fired in their resumes and cover letters. Most candidates didn't seem to know my age. The one candidate who clearly did—via a Google search or a press article, presumably—replied to the posting, "Is this for real? If so, I admire your chutzpah to post on the

Stanford job board." I wanted to reply, "Hell yeah, it's real" but instead I wrote back politely.

I never liked it when people praised me for my "nerve" when it was such a little task. There are moments when true courage is called for in a start-up life, but certainly not with such trivial activities as job postings. In general, people who tried to condescend to me changed their attitude once we started talking. It took time for me to develop effective strategies to channel age-driven skepticism into motivation (instead of plain anger). Whatever bias you might face, you cannot get rattled.

>>

I filtered through the onslaught of emails by eliminating candidates whose career skills seemed shoddy (cover letters help!) or whose experience and background seemed entirely irrelevant. Then, I corresponded with the surviving candidates and eliminated those for whom our salary range was too low.

Over a period of several weekends we invited three to four people a day from our remaining pool of thirty to our downtown San Francisco office (we shared space with Dad's law firm) for interviews. At Mike's suggestion, we drew a matrix in our notebooks. Next to each candidate's name we drew boxes:

- Energy
- Relevant experience
- Sales/marketing capability
- Teamwork
- Commitment

We weren't necessarily going to rank everyone from one to ten and then choose the highest-ranked person—instinct always superceded this—but we used the matrix as a way to ground us in the important factors. The person we ultimately hired ranked Number 4 by the matrix.

>>

Dad, Mike, and I conducted the interviews. I read up on employment law beforehand to orient myself. I learned what questions are illegal to ask (How old are you?), but how employers ask them anyway. I learned how to dig through resume-speak and figure out why somebody *really* left their last job.

Many candidates shot themselves in the foot early. Some looked at me like I was an intern, naturally focusing their attention on the two older people in the room even though it was *my* opinion that carried the most weight (since I was going to be working with the COO most). In my own sales experience, often the supposed "peon" or assistant in the room will carry as much weight as the senior person by virtue of their control over calendars, rumors, and so forth. Others, asked to "tell their story"—personally and professionally—chose to tell it in reverse chronological order, making their career story devoid of any cohesion or theme. A fatal flaw. A story that evolves and shows growth is important.[1]

We didn't try to pull any fancy Microsoft tricks in the interviews such as asking, "How would you move Mount Fuji?" or "How many piano tuners are there in the world?" We kept it simple: The first half hour the candidate told us his story and we in turn told him why the Comcate opportunity rocked. Then we probed deeper, trying to find out if the person was competitive, intelligent, salesman-like, and could operate independently. I favored off-the-beaten-path questions like, "Where and what do you like to read?" I figured each candidate would be competent enough and thus focused my attention on interpersonal fit.

>>

After in-person interviews, we narrowed the list to three top-notch candidates: Paul Elkund, Dave Richmond, and Eric Sigler.

Starting at 3 P.M. (after school) on a chilly February day in 2003, we brought in the entire advisory board to interview the three candidates. Assembled in the large conference room, I opened the meeting: "Thanks so much for coming into the City for this important day. I want to remind you that we're not here to pick the best of three. Rather, we're here to see if there's a superstar—by our

---

1 Everyone tries to tell their life story as just that—a story—with a series of events that naturally build on each other through choices. But my sense is that life happens and we react to it with little real choice. Even as I tell my own story, I probably credit "choices" instead of "reactions" more than I should. Yet we all tell stories to ourselves and to others to fit our preferred autobiographical narrative.

budget—who can lead Comcate to the next level. If none of these guys blows our skirt up, we will keep searching."

I then divided the advisory board into two groups: the ex-city managers (to judge the candidate's potential rapport with city managers) and the business folks (to assess his sales and management potential). Each candidate spent about a half hour with each group. Had we kept the advisory board as one unit, the conversation wouldn't have been productive.

First up, Paul Elkund. He was a fifty-ish gentleman who had been VP Operations at a venture-funded company that tried to sell a simple computer device to lower-income people. Like companies with similar visions, it failed. "After my last job I had to look my wife up in the yellow pages and then I spent some quality time with her," Elkund said, a clever way of explaining the few months of dead time on his resume while also conveying he was a workaholic. It made me laugh, in a good way, the first time he said it. When he fed us that line yet again in the big group interview, it became clear that Elkund had some good interview sound bites. My naiveté succumbed to these one-liners at first, but I quickly hardened up. Our experience with the interim CEO always reminds me that the more soundbite-ish you sound, the less credible you may actually be.

Elkund was an experienced COO candidate: happy to be behind-the-scenes, liked getting stuff done, worked long hours. . . . But . . . could he persuade? Could he "sell?"

I asked a question on presentation styles. "I'll tell you what," he responded, in a pass-the-salt tone, "I can sell this thing. I've done this kind of thing before. I'll do it again." His eyes looked to the floor for a second as he wiggled in his seat. I was so captivated by the odd answer I slowly turned my head to stare out the window, admiring the San Francisco skyline from the forty-second floor.

The second candidate, Dave Richmond, was a family man with a sunny outlook. His background covered important ground: strategy consulting, entrepreneurial experience, and time at a venture capital firm. He seemed dynamic enough to do well on the road pitching prospects, even though he didn't come across as any kind of rhetorical powerhouse. The big hole on his resume? Technology. No experience managing the software development process.

The final candidate, Eric Sigler, was a young guy in his early thirties who had just finished a stint at Goldman Sachs and was either going to start his own wireless products company or join a start-up. He was enthusiastic and willing to accept lower pay. He also had extraordinary technical expertise. But significantly, he had no experience running his own company. The question of a younger/energetic/inexperienced/inexpensive versus an older/experienced/expensive executive is a common dilemma for any company that needs experience but doesn't have a lot of money.

I stayed in the backseat during the Q&A, letting the advisors do their jobs and trying to learn from their questions. I didn't have the expertise to direct as much as participate as another equal. The group asked good, incisive questions. Ex-city manager Bill Zaner asked a particularly grabbing zinger that worked because he inflected it with tremendous passion: "So there you are, sitting there, with an *old* and *old-fashioned* city manager, who doesn't want to change, who's gonna take a long time to decide, who's gonna ask a lot of questions, who's gonna think you're just a grubby salesperson trying to sell him *dirt*. My question is, how do you *feel* about going into that?"

Dad was more concise: "Are you ready to be the first employee? No support staff, no one in the next cubicle. Just you. Can you handle that?"

>>

After all the candidates left, the advisory board and the core group—Mike, Dad, and me—gathered around the large conference table. It was 8:30 P.M. and our unpaid advisors were anxious to get home. The room still smelled of the cold sandwiches and salad we had eaten an hour earlier. Most people were munching on cookies for the sugar rush to keep them awake and energetic during the home stretch of the meeting.

"Well . . . ," I said, looking around the table, seeing who would step up first with comments. In an open discussion, the first opinion often sets the tone for subsequent comments.

"What, is there a decision that has to be made? Seems pretty obvious to me." That would be Tom Lewcock, always perfectly blunt and here with a tinge of sarcasm.

"It's a no-brainer," Tom Mulvaney, the former Seagate executive, added.

"The younger guy will be earning his experience on *your* nickel," Bill Zaner said. I didn't like it when our advisors said "you" instead of "we," because it made me more scared and alone at a moment when I needed these advisors more than ever.

"So Richmond was just that much better?" Dad asked.

"He just blew them out of the water," Lewcock said. "More charismatic, more fire in the belly, and relevant experience in the VC world."

People smiled. Maybe this wouldn't take all night to decide, after all.

"Now Ben—what are your first impressions of Dave? Your opinion counts most," Mike said.

"I liked him. Interestingly, he was the only one to initiate direct contact with me after the interview by offering to have lunch one-on-one. He recognized the . . . uniqueness of the situation, even though we didn't talk about my age," I said.

I then reminded the group that we weren't there to pick the best of three. We were there to see if one of these guys was TheGuy who could lead Comcate to the next level.

Thankfully, Carol Rutlen, CEO of her own software start-up, finally joined the conversation: "I really like Dave. I think he's a jack-of-all-trades kind of guy, just what we need. He seems pretty weak on the technology side, and we'll have to deal with that, but I see him being effective on the road and working with clients. If we're going to pursue him, we all need to realize that the tables have turned. *We* are now recruiting *him*. Ben and David—you two should call Dave first thing tomorrow and say you want to meet again to do a demo. We want to show him we're interested." I loved how she said "we," and I agreed with her point. The hiring process is an odd dance—who's recruiting who depends on the stage in the process.

After Carol's firm comment, Tom Lewcock, sensing that his role as an informal advisor to a kid with an idea had grown into one that was recommending the investment of hundreds of thousands dollars, added, "Remember, we're just giving advice. This is ultimately your decision." I looked at him, then Mike Patterson, who just smiled, and took a big gulp.

After people filed out of the conference room to start the long drives home to their respective Bay Area locations, Dad, Mike, and I drove back to our San Francisco neighborhood, Cole Valley. I've always loved these car rides. After marathon advisory board meetings we're all exhausted—and then there's the ride home for even more analysis, speculation, argument, continuing to the very last second when we drop Mike off at his home. When we reached Mike's block, the conversation had stopped. We were too tired to talk anymore. Mike opened the door to get out, and Dad and I both thanked him and said good night. He started closing the door, but then pulled it open again.

"Guys, this is going to be fun."

I mustered enough energy to grin. He was dead right.

>>

In between classes the next morning, I walked up the street from my school to my secret, undetectable spot where I made and received business calls on my cell phone. Dad and I called Dave to schedule a meeting to do a demo. His interest in Comcate remained high! We were still a long way from a done deal, but on the roller-coaster of emotions during the COO search process, this was definitely a good day.

That weekend we met with Dave at the office. There were good dynamics. Dave, at thirty-eight, had a boyish face and a certain exuberance that contrasted with Dad's and my more restrained demeanor. We huddled around a computer (no budget for a projector) and I did a detailed demo for Dave. I needed to be sure our COO would be comfortable and passionate about our product, since selling it in its current form was the Number 1 to-do. Surprisingly, Dave didn't drill down into the product. A lot of "uh-huhs" and "got its" as I went screen by screen.

"That looked awesome, Ben," Dave said at the end. "What kind of additional programming needs to be done in the next three to six months? Any big projects to keep it stable and working as the selling is going on?" To our knowledge, the product was as functional as it appeared in the demo. Only later would we find out that the piecemeal program our Bangladeshi programmer had put together had numerous holes. My answer was honest, assertive, and proved to be dramatically misleading: "No."

>>

After the demo, Dad and I took turns in monologue—touting the future of local government and technology. *Every* city was going to

Brainstorm: The Art of Courtship

How do you get "A" players to work with you? Court them smartly.

I'll use a cowboy analogy. When you spot someone you want to recruit to your management team, board of advisors, or even your circle of friends, you first have to throw the lasso around their neck. This is the preliminary contact. If you successfully connect, the long process of "ropin' 'em in" begins.

With my advisory board members, our relationships started with a simple contact and I spent years ropin' 'em in until they had psychologically committed to the company on a deeper level. I first met prominent retired city manager Tom Lewcock in June 2002. I immediately knew he would be a fantastic anchor to our advisory board, and in an ideal world, help us on sales calls as a credible local government voice. After our first contact he volunteered to do neither. Over time our relationship strengthened and I asked if he could join our advisory board, and he agreed. But he was still far away from agreeing to join me on sales calls to pitch his former city manager colleagues.

Mike Patterson, our main advisory board chief, had the novel idea of giving Tom some Comcate business cards so he'd *feel* more committed to the company. First, I got Mike the business cards. Then we staged a moment during one of our casual lunches with Tom, when Mike leaned over, held out his business cards, and said with a laugh, "You know Tom, you're going to have to get these cards now!" Tom laughed. At our next meeting I presented him with fifty Comcate business cards. At the meeting after that I made a bigger ask. Two weeks later Tom and I walked into a Bay Area city together to pitch eFeedbackManager.

I think Tom wanted peer validation, so we encouraged him to help us rope in another ex-city manager. We recruited his retired Palo Alto city manager friend Bill Zaner to join our advisory board too. In late 2002 when Tom told me he was leaving the country for two months I asked him if he could ask Bill to "step in" as an advisor during his absence. After Bill's "temporary" advisory assignment terminated, I told Tom we could try to convert him to a regular advisor. A couple months later Bill Zaner was on our formal advisory board.

Ropin' somebody in is not always easy. Dave Richmond and I tried the same approach with another retired city manager and Dave made the ask too soon. The manager said no and we nearly lost the relationship. Courtship takes time, dedicated focus on the real A players, and an awareness of the individual's psychological disposition.

---

need eFeedbackManager at some point, we told him, and if we don't act soon our competitors will. We were in selling mode to Dave Richmond. And we were succeeding.

>>

With preliminary mutual interest, Dave and I set up a series of one-on-one meetings to test our rapport. If either of us couldn't have a good time during a one-hour lunch, we would never be able to spend together the thousands of hours necessary over the coming years.

We had to get comfortable with the twenty-three-year age difference between us: I was an almost-fifteen-year-old founder and he would be a thirty-eight-year-old COO. Could we share a sense of humor? Could he tolerate my stories about school and me his stories about his kids? He had to get comfortable with the long-term prospects of the business. Is there a viable business model for a company selling a $10K-a-year software application?

We answered that last question in the affirmative after some scribbles on a napkin. I kid you not—along with the Laffer Curve and countless other historically pivotal doodles, Comcate's business model was initially verified as "filled with potential" thanks to a cocktail napkin.

We had to get comfortable with our personalities and our thought processes. For me, a difficult but important consideration when judging the potential of a relationship is whether there's intellectual common ground. This doesn't mean I need to agree with someone. It does mean we both need to have a similar devotion to rigorous, empirical analysis. We both need to appreciate the value of developing and defending arguments, and then conceding defeat swiftly for the good of the organization.

>>

My first one-on-one with Dave took place at the California Pizza Kitchen near the San Francisco Superior Court building, where Dave had just finished jury duty. My Mom dropped me off after school and gave me coins to take public transit home. We talked and ate and talked some more. We were clicking.

I was impressed with Dave's thought process; it was more creative than I expected. I have an analytical turn of mind and enjoy being around more creative types (who don't wear tattoos and have tie-dyed hair).

"Ben, where I'm totally with you is on the vision of making local government more effective. I have some specific questions, though, about how you're doing your implementations and structuring the sales process," he said. Dave had listened in on a conference call I had with a prospect earlier in the week and he thought we could present a much stronger postpurchase plan. Involving your top candidate in some of the business activities at the moment allows him to offer the most concrete and relevant feedback, a useful exercise for both parties. Dave outlined his ideas.

Fortunately, California Pizza Kitchen had plenty of napkins.

I then shifted the conversation to the personal.

"So Dave, what I'm most intrigued about is your supposed 'Top-500 World Ranking' in tennis that you boast on your resume. Are you just screwing with us or is that legit?"

He laughed. It's quasi legitimate, he said. He talked about his days of competitive tennis and the grueling workouts he endured as a high school kid. As an athlete myself with two brothers recruited for sports in college, I could appreciate his upbringing. The meeting ended on a high note.

Our final one-on-one, though, moved with a slightly uncomfortable sense of urgency. We were sipping hot chocolate in one of those San Francisco neighborhoods filled with Priuses, vegans, and war protesters. Only this time, no BS-ing about sports. Dave seemed more anxious to finalize a deal. He had been spending a lot of (pro bono) time with Mike working through a possible budget for the year. Before parting ways we stood outside the café and he said, "Look, Ben, I'm really excited about this. Let's move it along. You know, I have a few other things that I'm looking at and they're moving along, too." As I walked off to catch a cab, I could only wonder if he was bluffing.

>>

With all of us still positive about Dave, we did reference checking. When you call a candidate's references you are spending political capital he has accumulated with his contacts, so you only want to take this step if you're serious about filling the position. If a reference is anything less than bubbling with enthusiasm, you should be concerned. Dave's were bubbling. We managed to get an "honest" reference check from a teacher at my high school.[2] Her husband knew a partner Dave had worked with at Altos Ventures. The scoop: Dave was a good guy for start-ups, in need of a big win, and as we knew, weak on technology.

>>

The process reached its climax at our dining room table later in the week, where we all gathered over American crêpes for a dinner-and-working session. Dave distributed a proposed budget for his first year at Comcate if he were to join the company. Mike helped me interpret the balance sheets and income statements. It's important to assess the assumptions that drive spreadsheets. For his salary, Dave was looking for a total package of about $112K, which included a $90K base, 20 percent commissions on new sales, and 10 percent equity in the form of stock options that vest—that is, become available to exercise and sell as stock—over a period of four years.

While reviewing the total budget I suddenly had a dramatic change of heart. One bite of my San Francisco crêpe and I was fine and excited, and the next bite my whole emotional system did a

---

2 I learned that this teacher had an MBA from Harvard and sought her out. I did this with other teachers at my high school as well, even if they didn't teach me. Through my research I discovered an English teacher who was formerly the chief speechwriter at Apple Computer. I also researched what my school friends' parents did for a living.

180. I wanted to rip everything up and get Dave out of my house. I wanted desperately to be alone, a longing for solitude that's so intense it sucks your spirit out of any social interaction. I imagined failure of the most embarrassing kind and wanted to run from that image in my head. I wanted nothing to do with risking our pool of friends' and family money and our revenue stream—which all totaled $200,000—that was meager by Valley standards, but humongous for me. For the second half of that meeting, these inner demons affected my body language. I didn't say anything more. When the meeting was over, I cordially shook Dave's hand and excused myself to do homework in my room. As Dave waited for a cab home in our living room, I came as close to a personal meltdown as I ever did during my whole adventure founding Comcate. I felt like a boy who had wandered into a darkened movie theater, late, looking for his mommy.

I turned to my mentors.

I opened up my email program and wrote an email, bleeding with self-doubt, to my first mentor and advisor Paul Williams, who had many months ago expressed interest in Comcate's growth. In this email, I looked to him for advice, but secretly wanted him to submit his resume!

```
To: Paul Williams
From: Ben Casnocha
Subject: I'm scared as hell
Date: February 20, 2003, 2:28 P.M.

Paul,

I'm currently struggling with one of the hardest
decisions I've ever faced.

We are, as you know, searching for a COO. We're
talking with someone and we've had multiple
conversations with him (two interviews,
four 1-on-1's, another milestone mtg, comp.
discussions, etc.). He seems like a smart and
experienced person—someone who could probably do
great good and advance Comcate. At the moment,
we are discussing various compensation formulas,
budgets, milestones, and the like. A long time
```

ago, I think, we decided that we (me, advisory
board, my Dad) would like Comcate to go beyond the
cottage industry and attempt to raise money to grow
geographically, product offering-wise, etc. . . .
understanding that concurrent with that growth we
would lose control on a lot of the decisions.

So we've charged ahead and are getting deeper into
this one candidate—he's really enthused and so are
we (I think). We would be taking a big step by
incurring the largest expenses in the company's
history—right at the time when cities are cutting
back and facing the largest fiscal crisis that one
can remember (this is not to say current sales
aren't good—they are).

To be honest, I'm scared as hell—terrified—about
jumping into this ship and going from 1 to 100.
I mean, we started very slowly, growing slowly,
bringing a few more cities onboard, etc. Now,
we're suddenly hiring a COO who could bring on
many other people . . . and dumping hundreds of
thousands of $$ into it.

We have always talked about Comcate having amazing
potential and that the company can really go
places. At the same time, this has been—and will
continue to be—quite a learning experience for me.
Will keeping Comcate a cottage industry type of
firm expose me to the breadth of challenges and
issues sure to come up if we staff up, get money,
etc.? No. But how do you weigh a nice "learning
experience" with dumping a whole lot of money into
something that may fail?

Anyway, that's a peek inside what's going on
inside my head. If you want to offer anything that
I could chew on, I'd love to hear it!

Best,
Ben Casnocha

To: Ben Casnocha
From: Paul Williams
Subject: Re: I'm scared as hell
Date: February 25, 2003, 9:00 P.M.

Ben,

First of all, I think it is OK to be scared
sometimes. The importance of taking on financial
responsibilities should never be underestimated—
that's a scary prospect. You've got a great head
on your shoulders and it sounds like you have an
excellent perspective on things.

I think you are asking the right questions. I also
think you should trust your instincts—from what
I've seen they are impressively sharp. Take comfort
in seeking knowledge, seeking expert advice,
considering your options carefully, learning
constantly, listening, reevaluating, moving
forward, and making the best decisions you can.

I would guess you've asked yourself questions like:
What specific concerns do I have? What is the basis
for these concerns? What can be done to "insulate"
or protect the company if these concerns are
accurate? Etc., etc. Like I said, you've probably
addressed all of this kind of stuff.

In the end, I simply try to make the best decisions
I can for the company, given all of the information
that I can accumulate.

I want to help in any way that I can, even though
my time is tight right now. Keep me posted!

Take care,
Paul

I wasn't able to jump off the cliff.

That is, until Dave called the next day. He picked up on my
body language (an important skill) and wanted to check in to see

how I was feeling about the process. I denied having negative feelings about it (I didn't want to discourage him) but he knew what was up just as well as parents know when their kid had a bad day at school. I agreed to a conference call with him later in the week to ostensibly talk about the challenge of obtaining buy-in during the sales process but, more, to continue to make me comfortable. Looking back, I think my fear came from the enormity of the risk, the incomplete information, the emotional challenges inherent in an outsider's taking over the company—*my* company.

Brainstorm: How to Overcome Fear of Failure

I betcha I fail more than you do. Take that!

I failed to get good grades in school.

I failed to successfully start a radio station in high school.

I failed to launch my first business idea, which was going to be a sweepstakes clearinghouse online.

I have failed in countless sales presentations, sometimes with people walking out on me.

I failed to lead my basketball team to a league championship.

Now, I don't like dwell on my failures too much since I prefer to take lessons away and then look forward. But I won't deny that I fail early and fail often. And this is the best way to overcome the fear of failure: fail. Fail at little things. Get good at it. Laugh at yourself. Fail with 100 percent effort—don't engage in the kind of self-protection that 75 percent effort affords ("Well, if I had given it my all I would have succeeded"). Then when the stakes get higher, you'll have practice. There will still be fear. Fear of embarrassment, maybe. But with practice you'll learn to see failure as just feedback for improvement. For me, more often than not, failure means success got stuck in traffic.

It's not right to think you can eliminate all fear. Stress, nervousness, and fear can be positive emotions for smart decision making in high-pressure entrepreneurial settings. But don't let it cripple you—as it did me, during our hunt for a COO at Comcate.

It was a crazy time in my life. In addition to interfacing with Dave, I was on the road virtually every day doing pitches to prospective customers. In a two-week span in March, I was in L.A. for four days meeting with clients and prospects, in Los Altos, Livermore, and Orinda doing pitches, lunching with a professor who specialized in e-government, and on the phone with Mike Patterson every single day to talk about the COO negotiation. I closed a deal with the City of Cupertino, a big win over our handful of regional competitors. Along the way, I spent a night in Monterey, where I snuck into a nonvendor city government conference to network (they almost stopped me from entering), got bumped up to the varsity basketball team as a sophomore (those were the days when I'd miss school and race back from L.A. to catch a late afternoon practice), and finished off the cycle with a doctor's meeting: I had high blood pressure. At the ripe old age of fourteen.

Indeed. This all raises a deeply serious question: Did I even attend school classes freshman year? I have no recollection of anything of the sort (and neither did my transcript).

>>

Dad, Mike, and I agreed to Dave's comp and Year One budget in principle. By this time I had made up my mind to be supportive of hiring Dave, and subjugated my fear of failure.

Mike and advisor Tom Mulvaney were working on customizing an employment agreement.

"OK, Ben, we're almost there. I've spoken to Dave and we agree in principle to the numbers he wants to hit, it's just about structuring the package to get him there. It will be a combination of base, commissions, and of course, his equity," Mike said.

"Great—any deal breakers?" I asked.

"Well, there is one thing he didn't want to budge on. He wants his fifteen days of vacation."

"You've gotta be fucking kidding me."

"Nope," Mike laughed.

In *his* draft he put in twenty days of vacation and we reduced it to ten. In practice it didn't mean anything, but we felt strongly that he needed to know this would be a long-hours job. The fact that he would care enough to raise it another five days was mind-boggling. After all, most start-ups don't even keep track once the trust is established between the CEO and board. The only job is to take care of business and meet the numbers. But I bit my lip—as you often have to in negotiations—and we gave him his fifteen days.

We haggled over other details, like the specific commission structure (Would he get paid for deals that I generated but were signed after his hiring?) and the threshold for needing to get approval for expenses. All of our negotiations were done in good faith, both sides were reasonable, and I learned a lot in the process about how executive compensation deals are structured. Our numbers were negotiated within the timeworn "high, low, middle" framework: one side starts high, the other counters low, and we pick a number in the middle. This approach favors the person who initiates the negotiation since the first number anchors the discussion. The other way deals like this are structured is, "Fair from the start." Both sides sit at a table and try to come up with the fairest number from the start. No staged back-and-forth.

Thank goodness I had experienced advisors leading this process. Indeed, Dave told me after the fact that if it wasn't for folks like Mike he wouldn't have felt comfortable coming onboard. Moreover, I didn't have the expertise required to understand an executive contract. So, I tried to stay out the way, content to be the word processor. I didn't always have the courage to step aside when I wasn't able to keep up—after all, my credibility was important—but here, I did.

We sealed the deal on March 15, 2003. I had just turned fifteen. Dave Richmond was officially employee Number 1. I crafted an email to the advisory board announcing Dave's hire and I felt a rush of blood (was my high blood pressure kicking in again?) as I clicked "Send":

```
The day has finally come. When we started this
process a few months ago, I never would have
imagined it would be this exhausting. We literally
received hundreds of resumes from folks around the
world interested in our COO opportunity.

The diversity of the candidates was refreshing.
Everyone from young up-and-coming MBAs, to older
50+ tenured executives. Yet, in the very first
```

interview round, someone stood out as a winner.
Dave Richmond was the only person out of the many
we interviewed who, as I showed him to the door,
offered to have lunch in a more informal setting.
While seemingly a small gesture, that sense of
caring and kindness went a long way. Nonetheless,
we drilled this guy to death in the interviews
making sure that his impressive resume could
sustain the inquisitive city managers and business
advisors.

Today, Saturday, March 15, 2003, we sealed the
deal with Dave Richmond and officially have brought
Dave on as COO of Comcate. This is the biggest
decision we have made in the history of the
company. Dave is permanent and is our first
employee. We have determined that we want Comcate
to go farther than what we can all do part-time.
We have decided that we want Comcate to go to the
next level. Dave will, with the support of all of
us, take us there.

Dave, welcome. You will be working with some of
the hardest-working people you will ever meet. We
are all, as it said in the job offer, infected
with an incurable need to produce sustained
results. Dave—you must be, and I believe you
already are, infected with that same bug. You will
need to work your ass off—and then some. This is
in no way an easy job. The challenges in this job
are plenty. . . . The bar will always be raised
higher as each milestone is hit. We all have
entrusted an enormous amount of confidence in you.

I founded the past, Dave. We are both founding the
future. In the coming months, more than a half a
million people may be using our technology to
interact with their local government. The
implications of our technology, and future

technologies, could radically change the way government services are provided to taxpaying citizens. This is deep and world-changing stuff. Being passionate about what we're offering is an absolute must.

Obviously, communication is going to be key. Everything from directives given to Dave to coordination of schedules must be consistently represented and carried out. An important aspect that may make or break the company as we embark on a pivotal part in the company's life will be robust dialogue between everyone in the company. Honest and candid communication must take place.

In closing, I would like to thank all of you for your support and time. I would especially like to thank Mike Patterson for leading the effort, and Tom Mulvaney and Carol Rutlen for playing active roles in the postinterview contract negotiations. If our collective wisdom is right, Dave and his work at Comcate will be a success. Oh man, I hope this works out.

Dave—good luck, let this be the first of many exciting and prosperous announcements to come. Let's do it! Again, welcome aboard to Comcate. Godspeed Dave Richmond.

Very truly yours,

Ben Casnocha, Founder

Life as a Road Warrior: Making Memorable Sales Pitches

Making and selling—that's all any business is, really, from Boeing to the corner lemonade stand. The rest is dreaming, description, and distraction.
KYLE LUSK AND JOHN HARRISON,
THE MOUSEDRIVER CHRONICLES

When Dr. Ryoji Chubachi, the veteran Japanese engineer, hired American Howard Stringer as CEO of Sony, he knew interpersonal rapport would be essential for the duo's success at revitalizing the company. So they ran off to the Japanese countryside, took off their clothes, and enjoyed a hot bath together.

Our newly hired COO Dave Richmond and I had a similar goal, but instead of a Japanese hot bath we spent days on end in close physical proximity, mostly in rental cars, on airplanes, in stuffy conference rooms, in hotel rooms. We talked for hours about the business in between dozens of sales pitches. In our conversations, I tried to bring him up to speed as fast as possible. I didn't, however, want to destroy the precious window of time when his unknowingness made us revisit basic assumptions.

The two best moments to receive high-quality feedback from people are when they are hired and fired. At the start they ask many "dumb questions," which usually have gone foolishly unchecked for years, and at the end, in an exit interview, they can deliver feedback with the most possible candor. This is another mistake I made with our interim CEO: I inundated him with so much information that it probably squelched any fresh creative bursts he might have had after initial exposure to Comcate ideas.

>>

I learned a lot about Dave and he became someone for whom I developed a great deal of fondness. Our foremost bond, though, isn't mere interpersonal rapport as much as a joint commitment to the success of the business. Indeed, a great joy of working in a start-up is the intense camaraderie of the founding team. It's necessary and inevitable.

Camaraderie leads to candor. Early interactions were a bit restrained, but it wasn't long before Dave and I were blunt with each other. It was good for me to hear: "Ben, you know, I really think you botched the intro to that sales pitch." If you and your team aren't criticizing each other—if there's no gentle conflict— then someone's not being honest. . . . Or it means the team is not tight-knit enough, because personal bonds destroy the barriers to delivering honest feedback.

Despite our rapport, I still had suspicions. As the second business partner in my career, Dave had the misfortune of inheriting our doubts from our interim CEO. His first few months on the job I wondered whether a phone call gone unanswered meant he had taken the day off. I routinely called his office at 5:15 P.M. to see if he was still there. I questioned expenses and decried the quality of his memos as substandard due to low effort. My attitude resulted from the psychological heuristic known as the "recency effect," which says we give recent events disproportionate weight. In our case, they were the wounds left by our interim CEO.

>>

Before hitting the road that summer of 2003 after my freshman high school year to sell, sell, sell (and bond), Dave and I needed to focus our ground attack to maximize impact and minimize expenses. First we had to decide a geographic focus: How far away from San Francisco were we willing to travel to pitch prospects? We made it simple: if we could schedule in-person demos anywhere Southwest Airlines flew nonstop, we'd do it. This not only kept us within a one- to two-hour flight of San Francisco but also kept travel expenses down, since Southwest flights are relatively cheap.

Second, we had to formalize basic sales strategy that had previously existed just in my head. This included documenting the pipeline of prospects through salesforce.com, segmenting the prospect list, enumerating the sales process and sales stages, and outlining the various contact roles of people at a city (for example, economic decision maker versus influencer). We clarified our target niche, as Geoffrey Moore instructs in his essential *Crossing the Chasm*, because we were trying to dominate one angle of the market. This would enable us to leverage our focused success into other targeted segments of the local government world.

>>

My routine in preparation for sales pitches became predictable: I would spend hours at Kinko's printing PowerPoint handouts (to offer strong leave-behinds), manually set up each demo (I would spend an hour or more to customize the look and feel of the product for each city—it makes a big difference), research the city and its background (a rich customer profile with which to inform the pitch), and then visualize myself giving a powerful demo. I'm big on visualization—the mind doesn't distinguish between the physical and the mental. Management guru Tom Peters once said that presentation skills are worthy of obsessive study. In this spirit, I obsessively prepared for each one of my pitches and—crucially—visualized success.

>>

In addition to my personal, mental preparation, Dave and I spent much time brainstorming over each pitch. Seeing that preparation is at the heart of successful business meetings, we asked ourselves several questions.

First—who are the key players? Will the decision maker be in the room? Just assistants? A crowd of people? Sometimes we wouldn't know. If we had prepared diligently, one of us would have talked with our main contact at the city the day before to confirm the

Brainstorm: Presentations—Worthy of Obsession

It's worth it to be obsessed with effective presentation techniques. Unfortunately—or fortunately—the bar is low for powerful presentations. Most people are not good presenters: their voice can't captivate, their visuals bore, and they either fly too high or drill too deep into detail. This presents a marvelous opportunity to be extraordinary.

By becoming "pretty good" at presentations, I can come across as "really good" relative to the people who present before or after me at conferences or in sales pitches. I learned this firsthand at an industry conference. Watching two speakers go before me, I noticed nearly everyone in the audience slouching in their seats, eyes flickering to stay awake. I resolved to at least be entertaining. After a concerted effort to entertain and awaken (I told a beginning-middle-end story with conflict and humor), people loved what I had to say, and requested more information about Comcate's products.

Tips abound, but here are some keys to my presentation success:

- *Preparation and visualization.* Spend at least 50 percent of the time it will take you to give the presentation for its preparation. So if you have a one-hour presentation (sales pitch, speech, meeting), spend at least thirty minutes preparing for it. Preparation can mean many things. Besides the obvious, I find visualization quite useful. Visualize yourself in vivid detail successfully speaking and persuading. See yourself in your mind's eye being successful.
- *Enthusiasm.* Or as Tom Peters would say, "!!!!!" Emotions are contagious. If you're enthusiastic, others in the room will pick up on the vibe.
- *Beyond bullet points.* "Good men" go down because of Microsoft PowerPoint. Read Cliff Atkinson's *Beyond Bullet Points* to learn why images—not those circle dots—are more effective at communicating your ideas. Anchor

(Continued)

each slide in a provocative image and *speak to* the slide, don't include the text. For example, when I want to communicate the idea of "low-risk" I include a picture of a girl jumping into a pool where her mother will catch her. For "ease of use" I use an image of the Google homepage.

Keep in mind that the presenters who come across as the most natural and relaxed are the ones who put in the most energy beforehand. Steve Jobs looks totally at ease on stage at the Macworld conferences, but according to many Apple insiders, he obsesses about it for weeks in advance.

Never let yourself (or the audience) down. Take presentations seriously.

meeting and find out who would be coming. In a perfect world, the first meeting would be the "c-level executive" (city manager), his or her assistant, and the IT director. The manager's assistant is key; he or she makes the follow-up easier.

Second—what is the profile of the prospect? What's their budget? Have they been in the news lately? What are their pain points? What are the biographies of the management? Prospects love it when you've done your homework.

Third—what are we going to say? We had done the pitch a million times, but we always tried to customize our delivery based on the audience. We also reviewed who would say what and how we would introduce each other. Finally, we (tried) to agree on what to quote as a price. We never developed a standard price list for our eFM product. The price of the product reflected: (a) the enthusiasm expressed by the prospect during the meeting; (b) how optimistic we were feeling about Comcate's sales prospects; (c) how influential the city manager or city was in the marketplace (that is, a cheaper price for a client who might prove to be an opinion leader); and (d) whether it was cloudy or sunny outside. Many times it was a crapshoot.

This pricing practice drove us both insane—we had to write down what we said immediately after leaving a meeting—but we felt that we had no other choice. Each time we sat down and built a formula-driven Excel price list we never stuck to it because each case was different and each sale so critical. Given the stage of the business, we just needed clients to build credibility, so a few thousand dollars wasn't critical. We were fond of saying, "Look, we'd hate for the price to get in the way of a deal. Let's make it happen." In the meeting itself, we always smiled when one of us would launch into the quote and perhaps explain a "special" discount program or onetime offer. One of us might say a number different from that to which we agreed in the car, which always led to some interesting conversations afterward.

>>

One week during a busy July was particularly representative of Dave's and my shared journeys. I had arranged two sales pitches on Monday and three on Tuesday—all in Southern California. We met at Oakland Airport around 5:30 A.M. on Monday to catch the early flight down south.

Our first meeting of the week was in the City of Richwater, a small but wealthy community in the eastern part of L.A. County; a town nobody's heard of, a city hall that could be nicer on the eyes, and a staff that's not always enthusiastic about new things. This is what had kept other companies away but what had drawn us in. Disgruntled and ignored customers offer opportunities for companies that actually care to swoop in and dominate. I had received an introduction to the city manager, Jeff, which made the contact "warm" and properly teed up. Unfortunately, we didn't catch him on the right day. He had bags under his eyes, pit stains on his shirt, and a voice that scratched like your first words after waking up, except for him it was all day. "Hello. Excuse me for one minute," Jeff said, leaving the room right after he entered. We waited until he returned.

He then immediately volunteered the fact that his hearing is bad so I shouldn't be afraid to just scream at him ("I get it all the time"). I was determined not to scream at him, but I did raise my voice as if I were on a speakerphone. The dynamics of the meeting already seemed forced—as if he had taken the meeting simply because his colleague at another city asked him to—and I knew I faced an uphill battle. He flipped a paper clip in his fingers as we settled in.

I led off with a story. People respond well to stories. The story was I founded ComplainandResolve.com and my experience taught me that some governments were quite good at handling requests while others weren't so good. If the audience member nodded his head after this sentence it was a sign he was engaged and could see the logical connection between my past and present work. If he didn't nod, then he wasn't engaged and it meant I needed to ask probing questions earlier than usual. Your connection on the opening story is pivotal.

Jeff nodded, but without a smile. I debated for a moment whether this qualified as "engagement." I continued: "So over the next eight months I met with city managers, department heads, elected officials, and retired managers to figure out how they thought about customer service in local government. From the focus groups. . . . "[1] And on I went. I put that last sentence in quotes because it was what I said verbatim. At my best, I rarely had to think about what words I was saying. Instead I focused on the questions they had but weren't asking; I then pulled the appropriate stock answer out of one my mental drawers. It didn't take long to hear every question that's ever going to be asked during an eFeedbackManager pitch—the challenging part was spinning it slightly to the events of the demo or emphasizing certain parts of the stock answer based on prospect needs.

Jeff jumped in: "OK. Makes sense. So what's up now?" He wanted to send a message that he was short on time. Everyone likes to show they're busy.

"Fantastic. So that's the history. I'll jump into the demo in a second but first I want to ask you a couple questions. I appreciate your time on this, Jeff, and getting a sense as to where you're at will make this meeting more effective," I said. It's easy, during a sales pitch, to get rattled by an overanxious or overcritical participant. I tried to stay loyal to the format of the pitch I knew would be most effective.

---

1 When you don't have many clients to whom you can refer, the next best thing is to refer to the cities in focus groups.

"How do you currently think about customer service?" I asked. "How do different departments handle requests? And what are some of the priorities set by the city council vis-à-vis customer service?" These were probing questions. I think it's critical, before diving into a demo, to ask a few simple questions. Hopefully, you'll know the answer ahead of time, but if you don't, consider it useful information. Keeping questions broad may induce the recipient to talk a little bit, and with some luck you can pick up on that person's needs or first-impression concerns. Often I've found that a prospect has concerns before you say a single word—and they're usually unsubstantiated.

By expressing genuine interest in his work and in his city and not immediately bombarding him with a hard sales pitch, Jeff seemed to be opening up. As he talked about council priorities and existing protocols I scribbled in my notepad furiously while still trying to maintain eye contact. I took notes for our internal record keeping but also to show him I cared and valued his comments.

"Thanks, Jeff. That's helpful. Let's get into the demo." I had complete confidence I could engage him as I went through the demo, screen by screen, pointing out features and illuminating them with examples. It's important not to explain *too* much—after all, prospects who are interested in the product will want to ask questions even if they don't have any. Asking a question lets the other people in the room know that they're engaged and allows them to check their own mental box that they did the proper diligence during the meeting. So I always tried to leave a few obvious questions out there, only to come back with a kick-ass answer.

"How can an employee reroute the request from the initial topic the citizen selected?" Jeff asked. It was a good question. I showed how, after demonstrating the employee panel.

"And what kind of support do you offer on this product?" Jeff asked.

"Our support people are available 8 A.M. to 5 P.M. every day, and we provide on-site training and any follow-up training that's necessary. May I ask why you asked that question?"

"Well, for our financial system we had a bear of a time getting the vendor out to upgrade the software."

Ah, perfect. Asking "Why did you ask that question?" after a question sometimes reveals true gems.

"That's a great point, Jeff. Here's the thing: we don't work that way. Our software is hosted by us. Just like you don't build a power plant to get electricity, now you don't need to buy servers and use IT staff to use software. It's Web-based and you pay an annual rental fee. We're upgrading the software constantly. No more messy installations and CD-ROMS. We're pioneering this model of delivering software."

He seemed impressed, though he still hadn't softened his skeptical outlook on why we were taking his time.

"I have to say, I'm concerned that putting this on our website will encourage superfluous complaints. Why would we want to make it easier for people to complain?"

"That's a good question. We don't think that will happen, and the data from our other clients say that won't happen. In fact, our clients have enjoyed giving citizens better access to city hall online. Say I work during normal business hours; it's hard to pick up the phone and call or walk in and submit a service request. Now I can online. But just in case, Jeff, we've built tools to allow you to block citizens who try to abuse the service. Finally, if you don't want to offer the online service, you don't have to. You can use the product on an internal basis only."

I couldn't tell whether this answer satisfied Jeff's question, but time was short, and you always want to conclude a pitch under the allotted time, so I moved on. Jeff didn't ask any more questions. No more interruptions. He let me conclude the presentation, circle back to some of his initial questions, and then close by saying, "We'd be super-excited about partnering with the city. We want to make this work. We'd love to have you be our anchor client in east Los Angeles County. I appreciate your time and attention. Now, I'd love to get some feedback from you on what you've seen—what's interesting and what may be concerning."

Jeff bit his lip and studied the screen, even though there wasn't much on it. I turned to Dave, who had been quiet most of the demonstration, and he nodded approvingly of my presentation but seemed equally nervous about Jeff's response.

"Hold on a minute," Jeff said, and then he left the room. What the hell was going on? Based on his earlier antics and overall disposition, I couldn't interpret this at all!

He returned a minute later with Patricia, his assistant.

"Pat, look at this, it's pretty interesting. It's all about managing citizen complaints and questions and it generates reports and accountability triggers to make sure we're doing a good job. Ben, sum up what you told me to Pat."

I guess that 11 A.M. meeting Jeff said he had could wait. I did the sum-up. Patricia, the assistant, wasn't going to object in front of us and the boss. She professed enthusiasm.

"I'll be honest, Ben, your product blew me away." His face now turned into a smile, as if he reserved the smile only for special people. "And I would love to pursue this some more. There are many ways we could use this in Richwater *right now*. I need to talk with my department heads and I'll get back to you. Can you talk to me about the pricing and implementation?"

All right! But, for someone so intent on not showing his cards, I was surprised he didn't ask about pricing when he seemed less enthused. Had he known how wishy-washy we were on pricing, he could have gotten a better deal!

"Awesome, I'd love to discuss the investment." I always tried to frame "pricing" as an "investment."

Out of the corner of my eye I saw Dave look to the ground, so his face wouldn't be hit with the thick wads of bullshit I would release in a matter of seconds.

"We think hard about how to make the eFM investment attractive for small cities like Richwater. We would like to make Richwater an anchor client in this county, and we'd take pride in having a city as respected as Richwater in our client portfolio. So, for you, there would be a $5,000 implementation investment and a $10,000 annual investment. But, given the profile of your city, we are willing to halve the implementation fee. So, there would be a $2,500 implementation and $10,000 annual. How does this sound?"

"Well, it *seems* reasonable. . . ."

"One of our clients did a survey of employee time allocation after implementing eFM," I continued, "and found that an employee on the front lines is saving twenty to twenty-five minutes a day responding to requests, fulfilling public records inquiries, and so forth. When added up across the organization, we feel like the product will pay for itself."

"Uh-huh."

Brainstorm: Pricing in an Early-Stage Company

When I founded Comcate I struggled mightily with how to price my product. It's one of the most difficult decisions any new company makes (and remakes, and remakes).

Your pricing model will depend on the stage of the business and the stage of the product or service.

In an early-stage business, acquiring customers (at the risk of leaving some money on the table) may be more important than revenue. With real live customers you obtain valuable feedback, credibility in the eyes of prospective customers, and "anchor" clients in specific niches of the market. At Comcate, we heavily discounted our pricing to early clients. We called them "Charter Clients"—in exchange for the discount, they understood we had some kinks to work through, and that their feedback would be essential.

The stage of the product also matters. The early iterations of our product eFeedbackManager were not robust enough to prove a strong return on investment. That is, it wasn't self-evident that the product could pay for itself through efficiency savings. So, we had to rely on the more abstract benefit of "improved customer service" and in turn charge less for the product.

There are several other factors to consider. For example, you might number-crunch the cost of creating and delivering your product and then simply charge a premium. You might offer three versions of your service—a high-end, medium, and low-end version—and know that most people will select the medium version. You also will want to account for the competitive landscape.

The biggest mistake I see start-ups make is *underpricing* their product or service and therefore *undercutting* their product's perceived value. How you price your product affects how good your product is thought to be. Moreover, in their effort close a quick deal, a company that heavily discounts on a whim sets a precedent in the market and all other customers may want that "one-off" discount.

> All these factors make pricing an enormously complex issue, and paradoxically, one that requires rigorous analysis and spreadsheeting, on the one hand, and on-the-fly judgment and creativity on the other.

"A good next step would be for you and Pat to talk it over, and then talk to some of the others on the management team. We're happy to come back again for a departmental meeting. I'd also like to set up a conference call with your IT person, so they can be informed of our conversations."

"OK. That sounds like a plan. Hey, thanks for coming down. I wasn't sure this would be something I'd be into. But I can see why Doug recommended you visit me. I hope we can do something with this."

"Our pleasure. We're new to this area—are there other innovative, like-minded city managers who we should talk to?"

"Of course.

"Anyone in particular you could recommend?"

"Yeah, I'll email you some names."

"I'd appreciate it. Thanks!"

This approach always works to gain new references. I didn't ask for a "referral" per se—I simply asked Jeff to compliment a peer, so then I can go to the peer and say, "Jeff thought you were a really innovative guy. . . . "

By the end of the meeting, Dave and I were pumped. We had converted him from a skeptic to a cautious enthusiast, his secretary seemed positive, and he offered to refer us to neighboring cities. I was happy I had pulled off a good performance. An A performance. I luckily didn't fall prey to the typical B sales-guy shtick: Talk too fast. Get too technical. Marry my bullet points. Be afraid of silence in the room. Not take a deep breath.

After another positive meeting and conference call with Richwater, we moved the probability of closing the deal to 90 percent (probabilities drove our revenue projections). As it turns out, nothing ever happened with the city, and they inked a deal with a competitor six months later. The competition was fiercer than we acknowledged, trying anxiously to squish our upsurge in activity. They offered comparable functionality, aggressive pricing, and sometimes practiced unethical behavior (misleading our clients, posing as prospects to obtain proprietary information). At the time, though, we didn't have time to address that thorn in our side.[2] We thought we had Richwater in the bag, and we had to catch a plane to Sacramento for a client training.

>>

When you're singularly focused on one effort—like sales— something else is bound to fall off the radar screen.

Another part of the business had a series of leaks, and the dripping, like Chinese water torture, drove us mad eventually. It was, of course, the software itself—kind of important when you're a *software* company, after all. At the time we were still using the same single programmer from Bangladesh who did the initial prototype. He was the cheapest option then, the cheapest option now. Only now cost wasn't the sole factor: we needed a reliable system that we could regularly tweak based on feedback garnered in sales pitches.

When the application started creaking during demos, Dave and I immediately engaged the part-time efforts of technologist Edwin Dann, who had been playing a hands-off role on our business advisory board—until now. We wanted to transition meat-and-potatoes work to local engineers and away from Russell. Edwin was able to do some quick things to keep the product together, but he offered a stern warning, which I remember receiving during my lunch period one day at school:[3] "As the product has grown from the toy in your bedroom to an application with one hundred plus users, Russell has simply added code on top of a weak foundation, creating a product that's totally unscalable, filled with holes, and bound to collapse under its own weight, sooner rather than later." I was beginning to feel a knot in the pit of my stomach.

A week later I received a call from Dad in between classes. It didn't sound good. Sooner rather than later, indeed.

---

2 We did, later, when our corporate counsel sent a harshly worded letter to a chief competitor telling them that at Comcate, we believe it's more profitable to be ethical, and that we were saddened they didn't see it the same way.

3 To one early client I agreed to a service-level standard on tech-support inquiries that promised a response within four hours. This meant I had to spend much of my lunch period freshman year doing email.

>>

"So how did it go?" I asked Dad after moving into cell phone range. He and Dave had just finished a meeting with the City of Cortango.

"Well, not good."

Usually he was upbeat even in so-so meetings. Uh-oh.

"After the meeting the IT guy stuck around and asked if he could play with the application himself. Dave let him. After poking around, the guy accessed another employee's records even though he had logged in as himself," Dad said.

"Shit," I muttered. "So what now?" Edwin had warned us we should have redundant authentication to ensure this didn't happen.

"Dave tried to do damage control, but the best we could do is apologize and say we'll fix it right away. Edwin is on it," Dad said, with a sense of disappointment.

"Yeah, it's not this city that concerns me. It's this guy telling his IT peers. We're screwed."

"We'll have to see. The best thing we can do is follow up with Cortango ASAP and tell them we fixed the hole and then . . . hope for the best."[4]

I got a call from Dave on his cell phone a week later. One of our clients tipped us off that the Cortango IT director sent an email to the entire California IT email listserv, which said: "We received a demonstration a few days ago from Comcate. I identified a security hole to the representatives from Comcate which was pretty basic. I was disappointed." Can you imagine the work we had cut out for us now that every IT director in the state might have seen this message? This had become a full-fledged crisis: if city technology directors associated "security flaw" with Comcate, we'd have a hard time selling anything.

"I'll work with Edwin to fix the holes. We'll put in place precautions to ensure data integrity. What else do you think we can do?" Dave said.

"Why don't we send an email out on the list in response to the Cortango IT guy and explain the situation?" I said.

"Vendors aren't on the list. Trust me, if we could, I'd have done it."

---

4 We did end up fixing the hole and reworking the entire authentication system. We have never had another problem since.

"I could draft an email for one of our clients—Bellbeach, maybe?—and they could send it out as an endorsement of our work. So long as it's not too blatant, I'm sure they'd be happy to do it."

"Maybe. Good idea. Send it to me and I'll forward onto Bellbeach. It's just frustrating we have to deal with this kind of thing. Probably won't be the last of our problems until we rebuild the damn thing."

The Bellbeach IT director eventually sent out an email endorsing our work.

Later that week Dave and I arrived in Rosen City for a new sales pitch. We agreed to proactively bring up the security brouhaha since we figured the IT director—Laura—had seen the listserv. Our strategy was to raise and quell the issue before the management team arrived. We didn't agree on who would bring it up, though. So there we were, before the meeting making small talk with just Laura.

"Oh yeah, Agassi was electric this past weekend," Dave said, discovering a common bond of tennis with the Rosen City IT director. "Laura, I played competitive tennis in high school and college and it amazes me how good these guys are playing even as they've gotten older."

I couldn't believe Dave was bullshitting about stuff that didn't matter when we agreed we'd raise the security issue before the city manager entered the room. However, I soon learned that the direct approach had its own perils.

"Ahem, uh, Laura," I interrupted, already sounding awkward and startling Dave. "I wanted to ask you about something before the meeting starts. A contact of ours forwarded to us a thread on the listserv about our security. . . . "

"Who forwarded it to you?" Laura cut me off sharply.

"Um." I paused. I had already butchered it. What, was I going to lie to her? "Our client Judy in Bellbeach."

"Yeah, that's against the rules of the listserv, but I appreciate the explanation. I understand you've patched the hole. That should be fine."

The next day Dave informed me that our Bellbeach client had been kicked off the listserv for violating privacy rules. So much for the direct approach.

Brain Trust: Life Is a Sales Call

By Jeff Parker

When I started Technical Data in 1980, I raised a total of $100,000 to start the business. It became cash-flow positive in forty-five days and was sold six years later for $24 million.

One reason we were successful is that our organizational culture was focused on sales and marketing from the start. There is nothing more important in your organization than a great sales and marketing team. Revenues produce cash, which is the lifeblood of the organization. Everyone in the organization is important, but no one in the organization is more important than your salespeople. Create a sales culture throughout your organization. Get everyone interested in how sales are going. A sales-oriented company has momentum, attracts great people, and is an exciting place to work.

Good salespeople have much in common: laser focus, an emphasis on executing strategy, clear goals, and an understanding of customer needs.

Although most entrepreneurs realize the importance of sales to business, some forget its crossover to other life challenges. I often tell entrepreneurs, "Life's a sales call." Every day we have to persuade someone—maybe our spouse, boss, or professor—on our idea or plan, no matter how important or how trivial.

The sales techniques and philosophies that Ben and all good businesspeople employ are fundamental to forging your own life path and controlling your destiny. There will be many obstacles in your business and personal life. There will be skeptics and opponents. Your job is to persuade them to your side, or like a good salesperson, ignore the bad opportunities and bounce back and move on. If you have the philosophy that "life's a sales call," I think you will be pleasantly surprised at the results.

Jeff Parker is a trustee emeritus and a presidential councillor at Cornell University and was Cornell's 2001 Entrepreneur of the Year. He is a serial entrepreneur and has founded or cofounded several companies focused on organizing and delivering information to the corporate and financial markets.

I'm a Sophomore: Balancing Work, School, and Life

A lot of people ask me, "Why don't you just be a normal teenager, live a normal life?" says fifteen-year-old Ben Casnocha, having lunch on a cloudy January afternoon at a crêpe place in the San Francisco neighborhood he's lived in since birth. He speaks in an earnest, articulate baritone, and his vocabulary is devoid of the "um's" and "like's" that riddle most teenagers' conversation. His face has already shed its boyish roundness, and at a sturdy six-foot-three, he's tall enough as a sophomore to play center for the vaunted University High School basketball team. He has a game later this night, in fact, and he's dressed in loose-fitting warmup attire: stylish sweatpants and complementary sweatshirt, high-top sneakers, and a baseball cap pulled over his wavy blonde hair. But even with his size and his clean-cut looks, he evinces a thoughtfulness at odds with the stereotypical high school jock, and a lack of pretension that sets him apart from most adolescent intellectuals. "I don't want to be normal, I want to be something else," Casnocha says, his broad, friendly features curling into a frown. "The emphasis people place on the classroom," he grouses, shaking his head. "It doesn't offer nearly enough for me."
SAN FRANCISCO WEEKLY

Most hardworking entrepreneurs must straddle the go-go world of business and innovation and a personal life. For me, the "work-life balance" component of my entrepreneurship involved doing better in my academic classes and engaging in the bizarre world known as high school social life, which meant passing on the reins of control to our new COO at Comcate. I have older friends whose marriages were destroyed by their failure to achieve a suitable work-life balance. Somehow, I thought I would be immune to this issue. I had no idea this balancing act would make a single year of high school the most challenging of my life.

>>

I woke up late, so in a rush I just grabbed the backpack that I'd put down the last day of my freshman year, hopped in the car, and made the fifteen-minute drive to the University High School campus to start my sophomore year. I had arrived home late the night before from a full day with the City of Beverly Hills, a client. An unusually turbulent Southwest flight home proved a telling beginning to a disjointed sophomore year, as my body entered the structured walls of school while my mind continued to roam the chaotic world of the competitive e-government market.

"I hope you all had a restful summer," the head of school said, his customary opening on the first day of school, but I almost missed it, the sirens and lights and honking and cell phone all blaring in my head, drowning out most of his speech (though the traffic seemed to subdue when an ambulance—my BlackBerry vibrating—came racing down Main Street). I was in fifth gear at Comcate all summer—and it showed. I walked through the hallways of my high school in a disengaged haze. People probably thought I was high.

After greeting friends I hadn't seen for weeks, I unwrapped my new class schedule stuffed in my pants pocket. First up? Western Civilization: History of the Arts, the brutal interdisciplinary art, music, and history class. Oh, and why haven't I bought my textbooks? Gulp.

>>

During my freshman year, I could conduct a couple conference calls between class periods, exchange fifty to seventy-five emails a day, do one in-person sales pitch a week in the Bay Area, go to L.A. once a month on "sick days" for more sales pitches, play basketball

Brainstorm: Redefining the Entrepreneurial Lifestyle: Sleep, Nutrition, Exercise

What do you think when you hear of seventy- to eighty-hour workweeks, cold pizza and Coke every day at mealtimes, caffeine, little sleep, and the sacrifice of family, friends, and personal time, all in the name of business? Silicon Valley has created a lot of important products and companies, but it has also destroyed many lives and marriages. A balanced, happy life can accompany wild success, even if it takes you a while, as it did for me during my sophomore year of high school.

I believe that three small things are necessary for a successful and *sustainable* entrepreneurial lifestyle:

- *Sleep.* Overwhelming scientific research shows we need at least seven to eight hours of sleep each night for peak performance. Fully rested, my one hour will be more effective than your three sleep-deprived hours. People who say they only need three to four hours of sleep have probably not tried sleeping fully over several days to feel the difference. I have personally seen the difference in my own performance when I'm well rested and when I'm not. Believe me: I get far more done in less time after a good night's sleep.
- *Nutrition.* There's nothing worse than running to a meeting feeling hungry, or worse yet, trying to catch a flight with no time for dinner. Schedule time for meals. Travel with a healthy supply of energy bars. Also, eating breakfast has been proven time after time to be essential for top performance all day long. Don't skip it! And beware of those business dinners. It's easy to splurge on a fat steak, baked potato with the works, and a big bottle of wine (or soda), because you think you've earned it. And while you probably have, your waistline will soon reflect the impact of too many over-the-top business dinners. Don't change your eating habits when you're on the road—try to stick to your normal diet regardless of the situation.

- *Exercise.* I work out one hour a day, six days a week. I immediately feel the downer when I go a few days with no treadmill or weights. Many moderately successful, mildly interesting entrepreneurs work long hours and swear they have no time to get to a gym. But the very best people in the business world, I have found, always find time to get their one hour in. If they can find time for it, so can you. Again, when you're on the road, you've got to find ways to keep your exercise routine intact. Book hotels with a good gym, or ones that offer temporary memberships in a local full-service gym. Or book yourself downtown and do some serious walking or running before or after your meetings. The key is to plan ahead, and to make exercise a priority in your life.

I knew I had to redefine *my* entrepreneurial lifestyle when, for a period of several months during the height of my Comcate/school balancing act, the muscle below my right eyebrow would twitch involuntarily several times an hour. This kind of tic is a common sign of stress. After starting a meditation routine and focusing on de-stressing, the twitch disappeared.

Don't wait for your twitch to start. Do a personal reboot and develop sustainable habits.

year-round, read books for pleasure, get seven hours of sleep a night, and still do OK academically.

That schedule no longer worked, however, in my sophomore year. I was facing college-level courses, and my balancing act was failing miserably. I endured a string of steady C's on Western Civ tests before I woke up: *I will have to seriously refocus on school if I want to do halfway decent.* This is not a dream, I told myself—*50 percent of my waking hours have just been wrested away by the school for the next nine months.*

When a juggler drops a ball, she will come to this kind of realization—in all its naked truth—and try to hose it off, spin it, subjugate it as temporary. When the real answer to the question I received more than any other ("How do you balance school and

work?") was not what I'd been telling people ("I make it work"),
the disconnect was jarring. This kind of disconnect prompts people like me to try to partition reality into my different jobs: family,
work, hobbies, and so forth.

As is usually the case, it takes someone other than yourself to
turn the lights on and wake you up to your life imbalance. (See
why advisors and mentors are so important?!)

>>

I received an email from our academic dean. He wanted to see me
"in his office." So removed was I from my abysmal academic performance, I actually thought he wanted to have another BS session
about education theory and academic life, a type of conversation
I'd had with him on numerous previous occasions. However, this
time we didn't chat about theory. We instead dwelled on the reality
that my GPA had earned me the undistinguished honor of being
on the school's "academic watch list."

"Ben, how are you doing on your schoolwork?" the dean said.
He knew the answer. I was there for a reason!

"Well, not so good," I said. "Have you seen my grades?"

The dean was a little taken aback. Most students in this position are probably somber. I was straightforward and casual, for better or worse.

"Why aren't you doing so well? Is it because of your website?"

I took this as a cue to explain exactly what Comcate was
doing—I had told almost no teachers or administrators at the
school. People with only a vague understanding of what I was
working on sometimes referred to my "project" as a website. A
website is different from a software company. People not familiar
with a specific career often have trouble assessing its difficulty. I
have no idea what it takes to invent, perform, and analyze a complex physics experiment. Nor do I know how difficult it is to be a
teacher. Likewise, people not in business don't know how *hard* it
is to start and run a business. I wasn't asking for the dean to tell
me what an amazing company Comcate was or offer praise for my
work. I just wanted him to appreciate the effort I was putting into
it as something more than teenage Web design, and acknowledge
that as an outsider it's hard to fully appreciate something you

know little about. This urge to be appreciated for effort, even in the smallest ways, seems fundamental to human desires (or at least my own).

So I told the dean the Comcate story: how it got started, where I was spending my time, the things I was thinking about. I rambled uninterrupted for ten minutes. He nodded and offered many "uh-huhs" and "OKs." Then there was a long pause.

"Wow, this is quite the unusual case. I'm impressed. You've done a lot."

I smiled, hopeful. "But," I continued, "I *do* want to do a little better in these classes. I am studying for the tests and all, but just not, I guess, comprehending enough of the material." This was true—I was putting in effort.

"I think you're intelligent enough to do fine on the tests, but you are distracted. You may be spending the time, but your mind is elsewhere."

"Uh-huh."

"You know, there are things my office does to help students who are struggling academically. Beyond tutoring, we test students for learning disabilities. I'd be fascinated to see the results if you took one of these tests. If math has been a constant struggle, which according to your grades it has been, and if you are studying for integrated science tests but retaining little, then a learning test could reveal how you process information best and how you process it worst. Your studying habits may involve things that play to your weaknesses. My guess is that a test like this will reveal very strong capabilities in certain functions. The question is where are the deficient parts of your learning process."

Learning disabilities? The dean continued.

"Think about it. Let's talk again soon. In the meantime, I'm going to put you on fortnightlies."

I gave a confused stare.

"Your advisor is going to call your parents once every two weeks with an update on your grades. Your teachers will write brief summaries for your advisor, which she will in turn interpret and communicate to your parents. Nothing too formal or anything to be concerned about, but we do this when we want parents to know the academic status of their kids. No surprises is our goal."

"Yeah, I suppose I understand."

I wasn't thrilled about this. I didn't like a larger eye on my school activities. My parents, for their part, knew about my academic struggles and weren't locking me in my room. I kept them vaguely abreast of my grades as they trickled in. When I didn't tell them it wasn't because I tried to conceal anything, it simply wasn't top of mind. They wished I would do better.

>>

Why was I doing so poorly in my academic classes despite studying for tests and increasing my effort?

The first reason, the dean and I concluded, had to do with my foundation. Trying to "turn it on" midway through the year in rigorous courses that evolve on prior material never works (this can be said for learning anything). The second reason had to do with focus: my intellectual energies were often a million miles away. The moment something doesn't interest me I start thinking about things that do. Sometimes this is beneficial (it keeps my antenna to the world sharp); other times it carries me too far away from the task at hand. For easily excitable entrepreneurs, focus can be an elusive asset.

All the meetings and theorizing didn't change the end result much. I finished my sophomore year with a C– in math and science. In the science class, College-Level Biology and Chemistry, I entered the final exam with a C– average. I failed the final. I still got a C–, the lowest passing grade you can get without having to retake the class. I attribute this miracle to a letter I wrote to my science teacher, better known as a professional way of begging her not to fail me.

>>

Looking back on my academic struggles, I find solace in the history books. A lot of the world's greatest doers—preeminent thinkers in their field—recall school as a formal distraction. "Gifted" kids also flounder within the constraints of a normal classroom. Some people have told me that I am gifted, but I don't think I'm gifted like the children who start reading at the age of two or the students who find the dust patterns on the ceiling more interesting than the history lecture. I am gifted just as everyone is gifted—I have certain talents, certain gifts. Everyone has strong suits; some are just more visible than others. Some find those gifts early in life, some later on. The important thing to remember is we all have them, and for some of us they're gifts particularly well-suited to childhood precociousness (that is, an ability to learn and memorize information and then practice a lot to become a prodigy) or to adult precociousness (that is, high-quality *doing*, hard work, persistence, and other intangible factors).

As for me, my gift endowments seem more fit for the rough-and-tumble real world than the traditionally academic, and I'm not one of the lucky few who can be precocious both ways.

>>

Ratcheting up my academic performance meant I had to ratchet down my Comcate involvement. As any founder of a company knows, there is a difference between symbolically passing on the reins to a new CEO and really passing them on. You know you have literally passed the reins when the majority of decisions are being made without your knowledge. The relinquishment of control taught me valuable lessons about how to function like a board member instead of a CEO. I would ask Dave for updates on things, but never to a level of detail where it would seem like I was being a nuisance. I challenged Dave on ideas even when I didn't agree with myself, because if both of us are in agreement then one of us is redundant. He started winning more of the arguments because his domain expertise and recent time in the field eclipsed mine. In short, he was still putting in forty hours a week and my time commitment had dropped. Not being the hardest worker anymore—that hurt.

Our change in roles didn't preclude debate.

"We need to decide whether the trade show in Nevada is worth it," Dave said one Saturday morning, a regular time when we'd chat.

"Details?"

He filled me in. Conference fees, booth, travel, meals, and so on. It totaled to around $5K.

"That's not too bad," I said. "But we really need to watch the wallet. I'd pass."

Brainstorm: Being a Corporate Athlete

I believe time management is important to make each day rewarding and productive. But instead of focusing on how I can save a minute here, a minute there, I think about a different metric: energy. In *The Power of Full Engagement*, Jim Loehr and Tony Schwartz describe their "corporate athlete" system, which guides my life:

- *Objective.* Perform in the storm. Build the necessary capacity to sustain high performance in the face of increasing demand.
- *Central conclusion.* Energy is the fundamental currency of high performance. Capacity is a function of one's ability to expend and recover energy. Every thought, feeling, and action has an energy consequence. Energy is the most important individual and organizational resource.

Schwartz and Loehr discuss four dimensions of energy: physical, emotional, mental, and spiritual. I realized I was fully engaged physically and mentally, but not as much emotionally and spiritually. Like a weightlifter who will raise the weights slowly but surely, we must always push beyond our limits. For me, this meant exploring new kinds of relationships (emotional dimension) and rethinking my "spiritual" sense of being . . . which is admittedly vague!

Athletes also have an off-season. Periodic recovery time—disengagement—is essential to becoming more engaged in day-to-day life. This can take the form of a weeklong vacation, or simply just some disengaged time budgeted on a daily basis.

How do I manage and increase my energy? First, I focus on *awareness*. Am I aware of my energy level rising and dropping? Can I attribute my effectiveness to my energy level? Second, I focus on my physical dimension. Did I exercise today? Am I eating well? For me, everything flows from the physical. Third, I ponder whether high-energy interactions are worth it. A one-hour in-person interaction with someone takes a lot more energy than one hour doing email. Finally, I discover and practice activities that renew my energy supply. For me this includes exercise, meditation, and reading.

High-energy days have now become the norm, and I can immediately feel the decrease in productivity and pleasure when the corporate athlete in me sits on the bench.

"I think it's pretty reasonable, actually. We can get in front of most of the innovative city managers in the West."

"Yeah," I responded, "but what's our experience been at similarly sized conferences?"

"Well, think of it this way: at the California Code Enforcement (CCE) conference we paid $4,500 and got two new clients out it, which more than pays for that cost."

"But it's hard to tell exactly how those clients were obtained. Did we really hit them via cold call or email and the conference was a reminder? Was it really something *after* the conference that got their attention? It's hard to pin down the exact source of a new customer," I said.

"Yep, but again, for Montella we had no contact with them prior to CCE. Six months later, contract signed."

"Yeah. But what are our goals for the year? I agree signing Montella was a good investment, but haven't we conceded that the conference model isn't scalable in the long term? Are we really going to barnstorm the country attending dinky trade show after dinky trade show?"

We talked for ten more minutes, clarifying the year's strategy. We didn't end up going to this conference, but debates like this raged on throughout the year in a good way. Just as forests need wildfires to stay healthy, so too do small companies.

The nature of my chats with Dave changed based on my reduced role, though what they required of me stayed constant: focus, intelligence, and uninhibited passion for the topic at hand. All this came naturally to me. It was easier to talk to him than to certain friends or teachers at school. We spoke the same language.

>>

Comcate and homework weren't the only things on my mind that busy sophomore year.

I also faced the monster that cripples the self-esteem of many girls and layers a thick coat of cynicism on guys: high school social life. In other words, what happens when you stew hormonal adolescents in a big city. As an experiment, it's fascinating. For this reason, I often tried to play armchair sociologist when I could, but in the end I couldn't avoid the reality that I was just another roasted carrot in a feast of Corona, condoms, and confusion.

To succeed socially in high school I had to adjust my habits. I couldn't be "me" all the time. Even though friendships with teens preceded my splash into the adult world, adults and their style of living had become the dominant force in my life. Over the summers and during freshman year, while founding Comcate, I found inside of me an approach to living that was shared by my adult friends: serious, intellectual engagement with the world counterweighted by not taking myself or my experiences *too* seriously. But even in an intellectual and prestigious high school like the one I attended, this "me" did not always grease strong relationships with my school peers.

I endeavored to try to adapt myself to the traditional high school social scene so I could form stronger friendships—after all, I found most of my peers smart and funny. How could I strike a balance between my natural, more traditionally adult inclinations and those of my teenage friends?

To figure this out I followed my own advice as stated in the earlier sidebar on finding your passion (see Chapter Two): I explored the unknown. I went to some high school house parties, where alcohol and marijuana run the show, girl-on-girl hookups entertain, and, at the amusement of my African-American friends, ghetto chivalry turns white boys into Sean John–toting G's from the hood. Serious conversation is shunned in the pursuit of the hookup—hedonism and intellectual masturbation rarely make good bed partners, I learned. I went to school dances, where we all start with a common vision of an MTV music video but then splinter in a million directions, our lack of athleticism and beauty shredding any synchronized movement. It was an enlightening, if somewhat depressing, experience.

>>

I never dated anyone in high school, nor did most of my classmates. The one-off hookup—think microwavable TV dinners—is the new trend. My business activities didn't seem to help my romantic life; if anything, I think they contributed to a sense of intimidation (or as one female friend put it, "Ben's impenetrable outer shell").

I focused instead on building strong relationships with my guy friends by being clear in my own mind about how I would agree or disagree with them on issues such as drinking and drugs, two common activities in high school. Instead of denying a drinking-and-drugs reality that I found a little unpleasant, I staked out new ground on which we could base our relationships. Most of my close friends played with me on the basketball team, a commitment that forced us to spend a lot of time together, revealing common intellectual interests, shared humor, and a general spirit of happiness about the world—and even some lightweight partying on the weekends.

Whereas during freshman year my Comcate schedule raged uncontrollably, by sophomore year I owned more hours and tried to redirect them to building friendships with my age-similar peers at school. I wasn't totally successful. Maybe this is a good thing, since, as you may have already guessed, I found high school social life "broke" on several levels, and as Indian spiritualist Jiddu Krishnamurti once said, "It is no measure of good health to be well-adjusted to a profoundly sick society." This doesn't mean I did not form wonderful friendships—I did, and I thrived off our fellowship.

My sojourn into adolescent social life also taught me what my "personal life" needs are. And this, in my experience, is an important realization that all work-driven entrepreneur types need to have: instead of simply defaulting to bars and drinking buddies on one extreme, or the socialite life of the opera at the other extreme, figure out what activities and people allow you to recharge and enjoy yourself.

>>

In his landmark book *The Presentation of Self in Everyday Life,* University of Chicago sociologist Erving Goffman uses the metaphor of a theatrical performance to argue that each person in everyday social interactions presents himself or herself in a calculated fashion, working to control the impressions of others like an actor who presents a character to an audience. We employ different "masks" depending on the situation; indeed, our behavior in social situations, Goffman argues, is largely dependent on who's around.

Throughout my sophomore year I experimented with different masks. In business with adults, the appropriate mask seemed close to my instinctual self. I would layer my vocabulary and appearance with professionalism, politeness, and intensity. In school with teenagers, the appropriate mask—if I wanted to be engaged, friendly, social—was different. Not professionalism, slickness. Not "I look forward to picking you up tomorrow morning," but "I'll swoop you tomorrow A.M." Being "chill" trumped all. The prop change wasn't a simple swap. The teen setting required the same *category* of skills, only of different gradations. Pick the wrong shade and your voice cracked. You're supposed to be polite to teachers and peers, yet *too* polite and you're side-brushed as a suckup, a pushover, a brown-noser. You're supposed to be funny, except when you become too obnoxious. You're supposed to be academic and get straight A's but also be "ghetto" and loose. You're supposed to treat girls as equals and not objectify them as sex objects, but also confirm your own heterosexuality through silent catcalls at someone who just walked by. There's even another teen mask for those weekend drinking parties, where you're supposed to morph into a wild-and-crazy drunk dude after just a few sips.

Every high schooler wades through these unforgiving waters, kicking fervently to find a balance among all this sociological nuance. But most high schoolers are also placed in the right sea at the outset; they just need to figure out how to swim north. For me, though, it took effort to even find the sea. How do I reimmerse myself in the highly self-conscious environment of a high school cafeteria after finishing a conference call with a client on the cell phone outside? On the conference call, or in any business meeting, professional and personal aren't mixed. It's a one-dimensional interaction predicated first and foremost on the exchange of ideas rather than personal appearance, social plans, or dating history.

>>

What resulted from my hourly negotiations between these two very different realities? Well, I wrestled on the right mask for school about half the time. When I screwed up—when my nomenclature didn't match the social situation, when someone would spot me on a cell phone, when I would try to at once indulge and analyze weekend hedonism, when I would be pecking away at my Black-Berry in a class—my school friends just ignored me. They never asked about any business meetings. I liked it this way. They liked it this way. I'm lucky. Because until I could pull off the balancing act fluidly and successfully in each dimension, it was nice for us all—me, my school friends, and adult business colleagues—to believe in the illusion that I was just one of them. Looking back, I'm not entirely sure which one of them I really was.

Brain Trust: A Life That Works

By Chris Yeh

Entrepreneurship has long been synonymous with long hours and tunnel vision. Reporters delight in noting when the unimaginably wealthy still keep a sleeping bag in the office for pulling all-nighters (Dave Filo of Yahoo) or work fourteen-hour days (Marissa Mayer of Google). But what happens when the culture of workaholism meets the expectations the millennial generation has for work-life balance?

MetLife's employee benefits survey found that for this generation, work-life balance is now the most important consideration in career choices, outstripping the opportunity for financial growth and advancement. If balancing a normal career and outside life requires reaching deep into your bank account of effort and energy, balancing the entrepreneurial life involves emptying that account, taking out a second mortgage, and then borrowing an extra $50K from a guy named Fat Tony. How are you supposed to do it?

Fortunately, there's already one group of people who've had to deal with these issues: parents. And the techniques we've adopted might just help everyone (yes, even Ben) improve their work-life balance. Here are some tricks of the daddy trade that can help you balance your life.

- *Multitask.* Whether it's bringing your computer into your son's room and lulling him to sleep with the gentle clacking of the keyboard, or making business calls from the beach in Cabo, a willingness to incorporate work into leisure and vice versa allows you to double-book without cheating either.

- *Compartmentalize.* When you're not explicitly multitasking, compartmentalize. Establish that every day includes periods for work and periods for your personal life, and keep those two buckets sacred. This will also force you to focus on your top priorities in each category, rather than allowing a single area to run away with your life.

- *Find meaning.* Find meaning in your work and your passions, rather than seeking it in golf or other hobbies. There just isn't much room for frivolity when you're committed to a twenty-eight-hour schedule in a twenty-four-hour day. But that doesn't mean you can't recharge your batteries. Your work and personal life should be rewarding enough that you don't need to sneak off to the golf course or a bar to derive enjoyment.

Chris Yeh is an entrepreneur and writer. He's also father to a four-year-old son and two-year-old daughter. In addition to starting companies, advising entrepreneurs, and raising a family, he is working on a book about balancing fatherhood and the fast track.

A Silicon Valley Life: Building Me, Inc.

*You are the storyteller of your own life, and you can create
your own legend or not.*
ISABEL ALLENDE

By stepping back from Comcate, I lost touch with the day-to-day
details of the business and instead had two conversations a week
with Dave, when we discussed strategy, marketing, and product
development. It was a refreshing role change that I took in stride,
especially since Comcate continued to grow under the new hires.

With newfound time, I focused more on assigned homework
and studying. I also was named captain of the varsity basketball
team, the culmination of my lifelong commitment to the sport,
and it offered interesting leadership challenges of a sort not found
in the boardroom. And I wrote for the school newspaper, and ultimately edited it, offering yet another set of leadership challenges
that were rewarding in different ways than the basketball court or
business. I realized that while the singular focus on starting a company is exciting in its own ways, diversifying your energies can be
equally (if not more) stimulating.

>>

Despite additional school commitments I still kept a hand in
broader Silicon Valley life. I met people of all backgrounds, even

if they knew nothing about local government. I went to events on education, science, technology, and journalism.

What I was really doing, it seems to me, in this broad engagement with the local community, was creating and projecting a personal brand. I started living my life out loud. Many in the industry knew me for founding Comcate. But I wanted to be known for *who* I was more than for *what* I had done. My activities in Silicon Valley life fell into three categories: networking, philanthropy, and media.

Networking

As an entrepreneur flipped through some PowerPoint slides during a presentation to a group of angel investors at the Keiretsu Forum in San Francisco, my friend Carl Johnston—a sixty-something successful real estate investor—leaned over and whispered in my ear, "Give me one of your business cards."

I did. Carl scribbled a name and phone number on the back of my card.

"Call this man."

"Who is he?" I whispered back.

"He's a billionaire. You need to know him. Trust me."

And so goes one morning before school (7:30 A.M.) at an exclusive angel investment club that evaluates potential deals as a group over breakfast. By participating in a few of the meetings as a guest, I gained exposure to a range of businesses seeking investment. More important, though, I could mingle and meet the members, who tended to be between thirty-five and fifty years old, wealthy, and full of high-caliber ideas. It took a long time to get there, though.

That's because in many of my "networking" activities—that is, a concerted effort to meet new people, find out how we can help each other, and then stay connected over the years—I happily submitted to the laws of randomness. To wit, I did not set out with a goal to attend the San Francisco meeting of Keiretsu Forum. Instead, one day before basketball practice at school I engaged in small chitchat with an assistant coach, Max Shapiro, who is now a friend. I learned of his involvement with this organization. He invited me to a casual dinner in Marin County the following week. At that dinner I met another friend, Tim Taylor, who was also tapped into Keiretsu. The following two days I spent a couple hours with Tim. These members put in a good word and I got invited to the larger Keiretsu Forum meeting in the South Bay. At the South Bay meeting I met another friend, Carl Wescott. Several weeks later Carl introduced me to his friend Colin Wiel. I had coffee with Colin and stayed in touch. A couple months after that coffee Colin invited me to the inaugural Keiretsu meeting in San Francisco. Seven months had passed from the time I met my basketball coach, one innocent moment before practice, to the time I sat happily in San Francisco, munching a bear claw and observing the entrepreneurs' pitches.

Why do I devote time and energy to meeting people? Two reasons. It's fun and it's important. It's fun because people's lives are interesting. I'm fascinated by my friend who started his career climbing telephone poles and now is running a software company. I'm impressed by my friend whose father encouraged her to sell her body, but instead of listening to him she emigrated out of Southeast Asia to San Francisco to pursue her entrepreneurial dreams. And it's important because relationships drive business. Most successful people I know didn't get to the top just by outperforming their peers, they also outconnected their peers.

Once connected, most entrepreneurs are always looking to help each other out. I make introductions as often as I can—sometimes several times a week—if I feel that two people would benefit from knowing each other. I keep an eye out for interesting articles and events and forward them to particular people. Looking out for others in daily interactions goes a long way.

>>

As a young person with much to learn, I also was on the receiving end of these kinds of introductions. I sought out mentors and successful adults. I asked them questions. I took them out to lunch. I sent them articles and asked what they thought. My relationships with people in business, foreign affairs, journalism, and education taught me a tremendous amount about the world.

My "great leaps" in learning felt like when the players dump a huge Gatorade cooler on the coach at a football game. There were times when I would spend the whole game blabbing into my headset, and then someone like entrepreneur Chris Yeh would come

Brainstorm: Networking 101

The most frequent question young "networkers-in-training" ask me is, "Why would John Doe want to know *me*? What can I give to him?" It's a fair concern—after all, you cannot simply email somebody you want to know and say, "Hi, I'd like to start a conversation with you." You need a basis for forming a relationship. If you're a young person who's ready to "start networking," here are some steps you should follow:

1. *Know yourself.* Before getting to know others, you have to know yourself: what interests you, what your strengths and weaknesses, likes and dislikes are, and your existing commitments and schedule.

2. *Set goals.* You will only be able to meet a tiny fraction of the world's population. What kinds of people do you want to know? For what purpose? A long-term mentoring relationship? A new job? A new best friend? Industry-specific advice for your company? Defined goals change your tactics. There's an adage, "You have to develop the network before you need it." That is, you can't start building a network when you have a short-term need (such as a summer internship)—it's too late. Your networking goals should be long-term.

3. *Do research.* If you really want to develop a relationship with a prominent political journalist, for example, what is your value-added going to be to him or her? You need to acquire knowledge and/or experiences relevant to this person. If you want to meet political journalists you better be reading a lot of political journalism!

4. *Develop a platform.* Do you write for the student paper? Write a blog? Run a club or discussion group? Do you have a platform on which you spread ideas? If so, this gives a good excuse for an initial contact ("I'd like to write an article about you"). It also gives you more credibility. If you're a young person, a platform you *already have* is access to and influence within the youth demographic.

Adults want to talk to young leaders. This can be an effective angle when networking with older people.

5. *Think about the food chain.* If you're just starting out, is it smart to reach out to the editor-in-chief of the *New Republic?* No, it's probably better to start with a lower-ranking writer or editor who, if you get to know her, could introduce you to her superiors. Be realistic.

6. *Be self-assured.* It can be nerve-racking, but you need to muster the courage to reach out to people who are probably smarter and more experienced than you. If you believe that you *are* interesting and act that way, smart strangers *will* enjoy getting to know you.

7. *Assess your current network.* At a minimum, your network of contacts includes your social friends, your parents, your parents' friends, your teachers, and any other person—young or old—you have some relationship with.

8. *Start "networking."* Enough planning, it's time to begin! Work within your existing network. Ask each person on your existing contact list to open one door to another person for you. Then start reaching out to new people by introducing yourself and asking for something (a phone call? a meeting? feedback?). Be organized about it and don't take one "no" for an answer. Use your youth to your advantage!

Ultimately, forming and maintaining a large network requires time and energy. Like any investment, sometimes the payoff isn't at first evident. There are no shortcuts. Is it worth it to you? I say, learn to love it!

out of nowhere and pour a big bucket of icy common sense over my head. It hurt—the ice like cold, hard truth sliding down my naked body, like those early moments in the shower before the warm water comes—but it woke me up and sharpened my frame of mind almost immediately, and I came to appreciate it.

Mentors I initially met via a common bond in business I now know best through our shared pursuit of other disciplines. I always wondered if my readings and interests in topics such as religion,

Brainstorm: Networking 202

"Your network is your economy," Carl Wescott, an accomplished entrepreneur and investor, once told me. Once you have developed a network of relationships, your challenges evolve.

What should highly networked individuals focus on? How does someone go from being merely networked to being an "uber-connector?"

- *Authenticity.* Do you enjoy meeting new people? Do you find people's lives interesting? Do you find pleasure in social interactions? If you want to take your network to the next level, you need to truly enjoy relationship-building. It can't just be for the ends. You must love the means.
- *The "what you know" is important.* The cliché "It's not what you know, it's who you know" is true, to an extent. But as Auren Hoffman, CEO of Rapleaf, told me once, the what you know is important, too. Super-connectors become perceived "experts" in something. For example, I know some things about business and some things about education and young people. I'm an expert in neither, but to my business friends I'm their expert on youth issues and to my school friends I'm their expert on business. Knowing a little about a lot of topics can produce a powerful expert effect that makes you indispensable to your network. If you're interested in a nonbusiness topic, try diving deep into it and then availing yourself of that knowledge to your business peers. You might just become their expert on the matter.
- *Weak ties versus strong ties.* People often struggle between having many weak ties or a few strong ties. A "weak tie" usually means an email-only relationship or someone you've met once or twice with little real connection or reason to talk regularly. A "strong tie" is someone you would recommend to somebody else. If you don't know someone well enough to recommend her, she's a weak tie.

You need to have both kinds of relationships. Weak ties are comparatively less time-consuming and can provide help at unexpected moments.

- *Maintenance.* Connectors are excellent at staying in touch. Here are three maintenance tips:

  Set up an email newsletter to stay in touch with your contacts. I call mine *The Casnocha Beat* and send it out once a month.

  Send a snail mail postcard once a quarter via USPS.com (or any other service) to your network with a brief update. I once did this and wrote a short haiku ("Yay Summer Has Come/Business, Reading, Deep Thinking/Time to Change the World").

  Commit to making a few introductions a month between people in your network. Try to send a couple relevant articles a week to friends who could find them interesting. This outreach helps strengthen bonds.

philosophy, neuroscience, politics, and culture would help me in the business world.[1] What I learned through my voracious networking is that people are sick of the same old small talk and of the off-the-shelf, shrink-wrapped business discussions. They want intellectual stimulation. They want conversations outside the norm. My friends and I shared a sense of insatiable curiosity about the world, about what was happening, about other people we knew, about new articles and books and companies.

>>

As my footprint in Silicon Valley enlarged and my relationships grew more interconnected—when your friends know each other, it takes less time to maintain the network—I did more speaking and organizing. I spoke at conferences such as the Always-On Innovation Summit at Stanford and the Churchill Club Conference on

---

1 An October 30, 2006, *Fortune* article by Jia Lynn Yang and Jerry Useem suggested that multiple hobbies can improve performance in everything you do. "The more varied our skills, the more varied the neural pathways in use. . . . Embrace the irrelevant," the article says.

Brainstorm: Every Cold Call Can Be Warm— Rich First-Time Interactions

I get a couple requests a week from strangers asking me to take some action (look at something and give feedback, talk on the phone, meet for coffee). It's astonishing the varied quality of such cold calls. With the internet there is an abundance of material that can make a cold call more meaningful.

So, I hardly ever agree to talk to someone random who says, "Hey Ben, read your blog, wanna talk on the phone this week?" On the other hand, I do like talking to people who provide more color. Something like, "Hey Ben, I've been reading your blog. I share your views on religion and self-improvement. I don't agree with you on *X,* but would love to talk about it sometime. Here's some background on who I am. We also both know Joe Schmoe."

I still sometimes write cold-call emails to people I want to meet and always try to show that I have looked them up and do see real reasons why we should talk. Perhaps similar interests. Common friends. Common career path. Common reading list. Whatever.

Here's an excerpt from the cold-call email I sent to the author of the foreword of this book, Marc Benioff:

> I am contacting you hoping that we can meet in person for lunch after I realized how much we had in common:
>
> • I read that you started Liberty Software when you were 16; I am 15 years old and a sophomore at University High School and founded Comcate, Inc. when I was 14.
> • You have received substantial press coverage as well as multiple entrepreneur awards and listings; Comcate has been featured in hundreds of media outlets and I was recently honored to be named in France among the "25 Who Are Changing the World of Internet and Politics."

- You spoke at the Always-On Conference over the summer; I spoke at the Always-On Conference on the panel on digital music.
- You have the SalesForce.com Foundation; I have the Comcate Foundation for Teen Entrepreneurship. We're both interested in philanthropy.
- Comcate uses SalesForce.com Team Edition. I have feedback for you.
- You're a successful entrepreneur, you have feedback and advice for me.

I tried to show I'd done my homework. It worked.

There's no excuse not to make a first-time interaction rich. With blogs and Google, every cold call can be warm.

Leadership. I participated in World Affairs Council events. I cofounded the Silicon Valley Junto, a quarterly intellectual discussion group for high-powered entrepreneurs and venture capitalists. I moderated a discussion on microfinance and philanthropy at the Silicon Forum, a prestigious lunch gathering for business executives. Although none of these activities directly benefited Comcate in the way my sales calls did a year earlier, I felt these more general contacts in business and life would help me think about Comcate at a strategic level, could provide funding connections for the company when we needed them, and, of course, they'd be cool people to know in life after Comcate.

Philanthropy

Even if entrepreneurs just wanted to make money, their profit-driven activities would do enormous good for the world. Fortunately, most entrepreneurs don't stop just at the dollar sign. Although outsiders seem to view raging capitalists as greedy and heartless, Silicon Valley (and other entrepreneurial ecosystems) also promotes a culture of pure philanthropy, too. Launch parties, IPO announcements, and Web 2.0 conferences may headline the newspapers, but the Valley also plays home to books titled *The Business of Changing the World*, meetings on social entrepreneurship, and email strings on Third World poverty.

I tried to get involved in this scene as much as I could. I didn't have the money to make big contributions, so I contributed intellectually to issues I cared about. I started with a cause I could personally relate to—entrepreneurship.

One time I was asked to speak at a business camp for young people. At the end of their camp, I sat on a panel to judge the students' business plans. The students' parents came too. Afterward one of the parents approached me and said, "You have been a huge inspiration to my son." Thanks, I said. But then she added, "You changed his life." This really got me; I had never been told that before. Some say to change the world you need only change the life of a single person. I just smiled back at the mom, afraid any words I could utter would destroy the raw emotion of happiness shooting throughout my body. Philanthropy makes you feel good.

Why was I so moved? A future where young people are equipped with the entrepreneurial worldview is a future that's bound to be more creative, revolutionary, and conflict-free. There's never been a better time to be alive, and I'm ceaselessly optimistic about the future. That said, the world has problems, and if more people can engage in philanthropy in an entrepreneurial way, we have a better chance of solving those problems. After taking a computer-repair class in sixth grade, I was fortunate enough to have a teacher tell me, "Ben, if you continue to work hard and do well, you can acquire the skills needed to change the world. With education one can make great scientific or technological breakthroughs, curb world hunger and child labor, prevent the spread of nuclear weapons, promote peace, and have the power to bring about great changes in the world. If you don't change the world, who will?" I want to spread this same message of *empowerment* to as many people as possible.

>>

Giving back both helps out people in need and makes you feel good. I strongly recommend everyone participate in philanthropy at whatever level they can.

Brainstorm: Creating and Projecting Brand "Me"

Like companies, you are projecting a brand *right now*. Each of us is CEO of Me, Inc. The question is whether you are going to cultivate your brand to be as truthful and powerful as it can be.

Your personal brand consists of the following:

- *Your name.* "Casnocha" is a distinctive last name. "Ramit" is a distinctive first name (whereas "Ben" is not). If your name is "John Smith," think about a nickname that will stand out.
- *Your physical appearance.* We usually remember one physical attribute about somebody. For me, it's usually my height. For you, it may be your booming voice, your hairstyle, the piercing color of your eyes, or your choice of clothes.
- *Your work.* This is the answer to, "What do you do?"
- *Your affiliations.* This includes schools you went to, organizations you're involved in, charities you support.
- *Your network.* Friends and acquaintances.
- *Your online identity.* What will someone find when they Google your name? You should own the first result—it should be a personal website or blog that you run. You should also own an email address that is your name (for example, ben@casnocha.com).

Why is it important to think about your personal brand? First, don't you want to be known for *who* you are—in all its wonderful diversity—rather than *what* you do from nine to five? Too often we subsume our own personal identity to that of our employer. Second, wouldn't you rather someone walk away from meeting you with an impression that *you* have defined and that is helpful to you? When I meet someone, I don't want them to remember the name of my high school, I want them to remember that I sell e-government products to cities and also write a blog.

(Continued)

Your personal brand must—must!—be *distinctive*. A few months ago I was at a business breakfast with about thirty-five high-powered entrepreneurs and angel investors. We started off the meeting by going around the room with brief introductions. To spice it up, the leader of the breakfast said we had to say our name and our passions. I couldn't believe how many people said their passions were wine and their family! What a missed opportunity. There's nothing wrong if wine and family are your two passions, but if everyone else is saying that, then say something different. Suddenly, a balding gentleman took the microphone and said a few words along these lines: "Hi, I'm David Zack, I'm a compulsive entrepreneur, investor. I'm just your average guy with an accidental passion for the ambitious. I want to create things with impact." Whoa. I want to talk to him! Introductions at meetings are a great time to project your personal brand. This is not about making stuff up or trying to manipulate or show off; it's simply about articulating who you are in a crisp, compelling, and memorable way.

I once spent two hours strategizing with my friend Tim over my one-minute introduction at a big meeting. We analyzed what I wanted to communicate, the dynamics of the room, the needs of the other people, and so forth. Tim and I knew this one minute would be the first time many of the people "interacted with my brand"—and that first impressions last forever.

OK, so you want to invest in your personal brand. How do you increase its "equity in the market?" You are projecting your brand every day. It never ends. The people you meet (or don't), the articles you write (or don't), the blog you maintain (or don't), the conferences you attend (or don't), the book you write (or don't), the books you read and review (or don't), the stand you take on a controversial issue (or don't). Put yourself out there. Spread your ideas. *Act.* Ask an odd question. Get involved in your community and in discussion groups. Be a physical presence. Own your online identity. Love who you are and project it into the world by touching those around you.

Spend a small amount of time reflecting on what you stand for, how it's perceived in the market, and how it *should* be perceived, and then get out there and deploy it! Make it visible!

Media

If you want, the media can be one of your business's most important friends.

When journalists started writing about Comcate, the stories usually focused on me more than the business, but they still generated helpful inquiries and business for Comcate. Dave was always concerned, probably more than he needed to be, about Comcate's credibility vis-à-vis the "kid factor." If a newspaper article focused exclusively on me, a reader could come away thinking Comcate was run by one kid, instead of being a legitimate corporation with clients and employees. This tension and balancing act permeated all of my media interviews, and indeed whether my age was a service or disservice to the long-range strategic goals of Comcate drove an ongoing internal debate.

For young founders, it's worth thinking about how the kid factor can help or hurt you and your company in the press. For all founders, it's worth concocting any possible novel hook you can use to get free press.

>>

One afternoon I received an email from a young reporter at a local paper, the *San Francisco Weekly*. I thought I'd have coffee with him, he'd do a blurb, and that'd be the end of it. Little did I know that he would spend many hours with me over the next month—at school he walked around the campus, sat in our cafeteria, and intensively questioned me in a quiet conference room. At the coffee shop a couple more times he let me ramble as his tape recorder ran. He spent time with Dave Richmond and Dad. He called clients, advisors, and analysts.

What I learned was that for in-depth character sketches it's impossible to stay "on message," and that you're better off being as candid as possible. A journalist will appreciate this attitude and the tone of articles can be more favorable if the author *likes* you. No one likes being spun. I just tried to "be Ben."

On a later Wednesday morning my face stared back at me on nearly every other San Francisco street corner, from the paper's distribution boxes. It was a four-thousand-word take on Comcate and me. Emails poured in from people who had read the story. Some of those emails turned out to be useful business development leads for Comcate. Others said, "Go to hell and get a life, kid." At school, the lid was taken off a previously secretive activity. For two years I had told no one details of my work. Now, anyone could obtain the 411, and most did. The day the story came out I was eating my brown-bag lunch in the cafeteria and most other students—some of whom I'd never spoken to—were reading the article. Most of the guys were enthusiastic and excited for me. I know how easy it is to feel envy instead of genuine happiness for others when they receive praise, so I deeply respect how my friends reacted.

The *SF Weekly* article did remove an enjoyed cloak of secrecy, but earned this C student newfound respect from surprised teachers. One humanities teacher read the article and told me, "Ben, I have two things to say to you. Amazing article. And please, don't make me be the one who's remembered as the teacher who gave Ben Casnocha C's in high school."

>>

Then CNN called. They wanted me to appear on their morning show *Dolans Unscripted*.[2] I told them maybe, but that I wanted to talk to Ted (Turner) about it first. Joking aside, I actually did need to talk with someone before I could scream yes. I had a critical science test the same morning the producer wanted me on the show. Luckily, I received permission from my science teacher to show up a few minutes late (I couldn't tell if she was annoyed or amused).

I arrived at 6 A.M. at CNN's San Francisco bureau on a chilly Thursday morning. I was escorted to the room where I would have the interview with Ken and Daria, who were in New York City. My vision of a fancy studio with all sorts of cameras and lights clashed with the reality—a cramped little room housing just two cameras and dirty walls. Of course, the wall that counted—the one behind my chair—sparkled with a skyline of San Francisco. It was painted to make it seem like I was sitting in front of an expansive glass window overlooking San Francisco's downtown. I settled into my seat and awaited further instructions. The technician installed my earpiece, adjusted my chair height, and checked my invisible microphone. After that, he said "Good luck!" and left the room. Perplexed, I sat for a few minutes staring at the TV screen to my right that showed

---

2 To see the interview visit www.mystartuplife.com.

the Dolans' show live. They had just started. Suddenly I heard a voice in my earpiece.

"Hi Ben, this is Jim. I'm the tech producer for your segment in CNN's New York City studios. Can you hear me all right?"

"I sure can."

"Great. Listen, I'm controlling the camera in front of you, your microphone, and your earpiece volume. I'm going to do a series of tests to make sure you are all set. Your segment will be on the air in approximately thirteen minutes."

I was awestruck that the producers in New York City controlled the cameras and lights remotely. There was a bit of silence, and I refocused my attention to the TV. The Dolans were interviewing an expert on presidential communications who was comparing John Kerry and George W. Bush. A different voice came on my earpiece.

"Hi Ben—this is Stephanie, the segment producer. How are you feeling? Are you all set to go?"

"I am—thanks again for having me on the show."

"You bet. Be sure to take a deep breath, relax, and speak slowly while staring directly into the eye of the camera in front of you. I've briefed Ken and Daria, and they are excited to talk with you. Have fun!"

A few more tense minutes went by and then the TV monitor in my room went off. The technician must have turned it off so I wouldn't be distracted. There is a slight delay between one's words and their appearance live on TV.

"Ben—this is Jim. You're going on in 10, 9, . . . 5, 4, 3, 2, 1. . . . "

Then I heard the show's theme music play into my earpiece and I knew my mic was hot. I heard Ken and Daria introduce the segment and ask the first question and I stared into the dark eye of the camera, pretended it was a face, and smiled. . . . A few minutes later it was all over!

>>

After each media appearance I would receive many emails from strangers. Most of them were quite kind. Some weren't. And sometimes I received messages that were not so easily classified. One time, for example, I got a voicemail from a young woman who, after seeing a TV interview, asked me to perform a sexual act on her. I played the message to an older girl acquaintance, a senior, on the bus to the gym that day, and later that night she called and asked if I, a sophomore, could accompany her to the junior/senior prom. (Whatever it takes!)

It is important to know when to say no. (I'm talking about requests for media appearances, not requests for sexual favors.) Some media exposure might actually be bad publicity. MTV once called me and wanted to feature me in their show called *True Life,* a minidocumentary on young people. After discussing the theme for their show ("I Don't Fit In") and the bios of the other subjects, I decided it wouldn't be a good venue for me. A good move—when the show aired a few months later the other profilees were bizarre and not people I would like to be compared to.

When you interact with the media you give up privacy, though for me "transparency" (and press) has always outweighed any loss of privacy. But transparency doesn't come without costs. I still get hate mail. Weigh the costs and benefits yourself before plunging into a media plan.

>>

My active involvement in Silicon Valley life taught me that many people are starved for something *different.* To become respected in a community you have to add value, and one way to do this is to be different. Being smart is not enough. Smart is like vanilla ice cream. For me, I tried to offer different ideas, acquire different experiences, and learn about different fields. I sought out different kinds of people. And by exposing myself to this kind of randomness, I felt able to contribute—by connecting ideas and people—in a community that boasts minds more brilliant than my own.

The Product Development Process: Cheap, Good, or Fast?

The problem with communication . . . is the illusion *that it has been accomplished.*
GEORGE BERNARD SHAW

"He's *what?* He's quitting on us?" I asked over the noise of basketballs bouncing inside.

I couldn't believe it. Since when does a consultant fire *you?* Dave had just told me Edwin Dann, our part-time chief technology officer, announced he wanted nothing more to do with Comcate. I was sitting outside the San Francisco YMCA. I went to the gym with my friends after school and I told them to go ahead inside and that I'd join them later. Two hours later, they walked out of the gym, dripping in sweat, and I was still sitting on the bench on the phone, in a different kind of sweat—the cold sort, seeping through pores of disbelief and nervousness.

And so began an around-the-clock effort to retain our programmers and get our product development process back on track. The challenges we faced in the coming weeks reveal lessons about communication, expectations, and trade-offs applicable to all businesses balancing the different working styles of team members.

>>

For a software company to grow and add clients, the software itself has to be scalable to accommodate increased product use. Just as the all-wood foundation of a house will come back to haunt you in an earthquake (I'm a San Franciscan, remember!), a shoddy foundation of a product will last only so long. The programmer will express repeated concern over the long-term risks of the architecture while the entrepreneur—or homeowner—will keep wanting to add new stuff. At Comcate, we still relied on Russell's version .05 prototype as the main system on which our client base relied, and while it was a fine setup for beta testers, it wasn't suitable for five or ten active governments using the software.

Like so many challenges in business, this one reared its head not in a technical sense—the product did *not* implode as we feared—but in a human sense. It's about people, in the end. And the people involved in our product development process felt alienated. The technical folks—led by our CTO Edwin Dann—believed the business folks (Dave and me) didn't grasp the nature of the technology. They believed we made too many unrealistic demands regarding what product functionality could be developed and at what cost. The business folks thought the engineers were unnecessarily vague in their time line and cost estimates ("It's done when it's done" always justifiably infuriates managers who need to stick to a budget). These interpersonal tensions led Edwin to tell Dave: "I want out."

>>

"So what did he say? What was his rationale?" I asked Dave outside the YMCA, slightly peeved that he had given no prior indication of Edwin's discontent.

"He said our development process is broken. And that me and him aren't seeing eye-to-eye on enough things. He said we have too many different people working on each new version and no one person responsible for the overall vision and functionality of the product. He's sick of dealing with changing priorities. He's sick of reactionary product development. And his last big point was on Bangladesh. He said we need to commit to a stable product, and basically, have some balls and rebuild the thing and take pride in the work. And stop screwing around with Russell."

All fair points. Our product development was haphazard, spanning three time zones and five different people, none of whom had total responsibility or accountability for the work.

"That sound reasonable," I told Dave. "I mean, it seems like our Christmas fiasco was the forbearer to all this."

"Yes, it does," Dave said glumly.

Christmas Eve 2003 was the perfect symbol for this dark realization that our software development had hit rock bottom. Instead of sipping eggnog by the mistletoe, Dave and I were emailing and instant messaging our engineers in Shanghai, furiously trying to describe what updates in the product we needed. We had to convert a general request from the customer into detailed, technical specifications—and I mean *really* detailed, because that's what it takes when you're dealing with inexpensive offshore people. (Technology start-ups take note: when a programmer isn't on the founding team, it is difficult to find engineers who are both high quality and affordable.)

"But Dave, while these seem like reasonable *concerns,* why is he quitting on us? Shouldn't we talk about them and try to work through them? I think they're solvable. Edwin leaving would make us too vulnerable to the offshore guys and could really screw us in the short term."

He didn't have a good answer. Edwin and he had hit a wall and it occurred to me that while all of the concerns about outsourcing and flawed processes were valid, what had really happened was the Dave-Edwin personal relationship had collapsed.

>>

I talked with my advisory board to strategize on what we should do. Edwin wanted out. Dave presented other non-Edwin IT options. I, though, felt strongly we had to keep Edwin even at a significant cost. For one, I reluctantly agreed with Edwin that we needed to give him (or somebody) ultimate responsibility to develop the product. Second, he had accumulated institutional knowledge about the product that would take months to replace in a new CTO. We had too many programming needs to let a few months pass for a new guy to get up to speed. Dave came onboard with this perspective, and together, we set to work to reengage a frustrated Edwin.

First, we focused on *repairing the relationship*. The Comcate-Edwin–offshore programmers relationship had disintegrated. We questioned each others' motives, challenged billable hours, and pointed fingers when something didn't come in on time. Dad and I scheduled an in-person meeting with Edwin (a too-rare occurrence given that we lived only an hour away) and communicated our appreciation for his work. We told him how important he was to the success of the company and that we were committed to retaining him, despite his intent to quit (he thought it was a decision—we called it "intent").

Second, we *confronted the root of the problem*. When something is hard, frustration is right around the corner. When something is frustrating, communication breakdowns are right around the next corner. And when communications break down, shit is going to hit the fan. Are communication breakdowns inevitable? No matter what industry or context, I believe a so-called communication breakdown really has to do with "expectation mismanagement." People aren't on the same page. One person thinks something is going to be done by a certain day, but the person actually completing the task has a different deadline in mind. The business executive budgets $X for a specific release, and the engineers come in over budget.

The first step to remedying communication breakdowns is to make sure everyone's expectations are aligned, and this means memorializing all expectations on paper. Edwin agreed that poor communication and differing expectations belittled both the actual product and the human relationships that held it together. In this meeting, both sides agreed on the centrality of aligned expectations and we both committed to clear, frequent, in-person communication.

Third, we *made concessions and new requests*. We conceded our own misjudgments in thinking an outsourced, on-the-cheap product development process could work. We committed to giving Edwin and his local team 100 percent control and accountability on the product development (this meant a big boost in the technology budget). In exchange for these concessions, we requested Edwin invest his own time and emotional energy into our projects, manage any of our offshore partners, take the lead role in the product management work (marketing requirements documents and the like), and participate at a strategic level during management team meetings.

Through this three-pronged approach—respect and repair, confront the brutal reality, concede and propose new terms—we retained Edwin and his team as the full-time technology engineering group for Comcate.

>>

Many people ask how a software company could let the actual software development unravel as it did. Isn't developing software the core competency of the business? It's actually not that simple. In the early goings, it can be better to ship less-than-perfect software and focus on selling, selling, selling, rather than making perfect software. This stands true for many products, I think. Better to have a product earn some battle scars from real customers in the field than sit in a manufacturing plant or laboratory while kinks are worked out. So getting good at product development didn't

---

Brainstorm: Dare to Be Mediocre:
Good Is the Enemy of Perfect

Sometimes A students have difficulty being entrepreneurs. Why? Because effective entrepreneurs accept "good enough." Good enough means not trying eighty different fonts on the brochure. Good enough means pleasing your customers without adding features or services they don't care about. Going from a B+ to A+ means falling prey to diminishing marginal returns.

Good is the enemy of perfect most strikingly in the product development process. When we endured our software development debacles we had to make difficult decisions about whether to add certain features to our product. If we weren't thinking straight, we'd add a "cool" feature that less than 10 percent of our users would need. A mediocre graphic instead of an interactive one on that little-used report, for example, would be just fine.

(Continued)

So when you do strive for "great?" You don't want "frugality creep" to make *everything* about your efforts seem mediocre. The challenge is figuring out which decisions call for good enough versus great.

Here's a company that's found the balance: Google. Google's food for employees is terrific. The chairs and tables on which they eat are pathetic. They cut the right corners. They're mediocre in the right places. They're not mediocre, for instance, when it comes to values ("Don't be evil"). Who would settle for "good" and say "Don't be evil *most of the time?*"

At Comcate we were once preparing a response to a request for proposals. The RFP was twenty-five pages long and asked for what seemed like extraneous information. Nevertheless, we slaved away, carefully preparing each section, debating the content of the introduction and conclusion, and second-guessing our choice of graphics. After an entire afternoon on the job, my partners and I looked at each other. "*Why*, exactly, are we spending so much time tweaking this one response?" said Olivier Marchand, our director of client services. It's what we were all thinking. Our sixty-page response, in its current iteration, communicated the necessities just fine.

"Good enough," I said.

"Good enough," Dave said.

"Good enough," Olivier said, with a smile.

And we moved on. Three weeks later, we were awarded a $40,000 contract.

become a priority until it fell apart. . . . And while I wish we would have addressed the issue proactively by ignoring sunk costs and rebuilding the product from scratch, and I wish we would have done a better job at managing the relationship with our engineers, in one sense we did what we had to do given the tight cash resources: sign new deals, even if it meant overpromising a bit or putting excessive strain on our servers. Or nearly losing our CTO.

When it finally caught up with us, in early 2004, we halted most sales activity to focus on IT. Boy, did we feel the financial squeeze of reduced revenue and increased development expenses.

>>

Product development in an early-stage business is full of trade-offs. Do you want it cheap, fast, or good? Choose two, says the old engineering adage. A newly matured Comcate chose high-quality and fast (*and* expensive) product development—a move our customers have appreciated ever since.

But we nearly drowned in the process.

It's a Frugal, Frugal World: Bootstrapping Through the Inevitable Cash Squeeze

The trouble with simple living is that, though it can be joyful, rich, and creative, it isn't simple.
DORIS JANZEN LONGACRE

"OK, sir, hold out your arms."

The barely-English-speaking Transportation Security Administration officer had his metal detector and slid it from my left ankle up to my left armpit and back down the other side. I sighed, patiently. A little hassle is worth the double Southwest Airlines Rapid Rewards credit. During a promotional period Southwest awarded double flight credit if you booked online. You could only book one-way tickets online. So, I booked two one-ways online, earned double credit, and only had to endure the extra security screening given to one-way ticket passengers.

>>

"Well, at least there's a bed."

Dad made the first comment as we both entered a barren, disgusting hotel room in Moreno Valley, California, where I was pitching the city the following morning. The room had no desk, a meager dresser, and two brown stains on the faded blue carpet.

But, it had a bed. We were lucky we even got a room; the bumbling hotel front desk staff person did not accept any of our credit cards.

>>

"Please sign here and we'll get you on the way to the shuttle in just a moment."

"Another shuttle?" I exclaimed. "We've already been on two!"

"Yes, sir, we need to take you to the actual car lot."

I had reserved a rental car for Mom and me for one of my L.A. sales trips and thought I had snagged a deal with Advantage Rent-a-Car at $35 a day. After arriving in Ontario International Airport, we took a shuttle to the car rental station, then a shuttle to the Advantage Rent-a-Car office, and now a third shuttle to the car lot. All in all, two and a half hours elapsed between deplaning and driving away in a rental car.

>>

"Let's see. Ink jet would cost $54 and the laser $125. Tell me why you think laser is better?" I said.

Dave and I were debating what kind of printer he should buy. It was a representative decision of hard cost-cutting efforts: ink jet is cheaper in the short term, but more expensive in the long run. Most technology purchases pose this difficulty. The less expensive computer model may save money now, but when it breaks down in six months, it wouldn't have been worth it. These trade-offs can befuddle start-ups.

>>

"Oh no, don't open your mouth, don't you say a word!"

My junior high school teacher knew why I had arrived at his office with a grin on my face. I wanted, once again, to borrow the school's projector for my early Comcate presentations. I had yet to invest in my own projector because of the prohibitive cost. Borrowing other people's stuff worked just fine.

>>

"Hertz, Hertz, Hertz. Doesn't Dave get it? Hertz is *the* most expensive car rental company, and yet he rents from there each time. Doesn't he get that we are *not* a Hertz kind of company, yet?"

Dad was venting to me over another Dave Richmond expense report. Not only did the car rental expenses raise an eyebrow, but Dad noticed a Southern California restaurant meal on the same day Dave claimed to be in Marin County. Naturally, Dad wrote Dave an email, requesting clarification on various items:

```
Dear Dave,


I was surprised to see yet another Hertz bill
on your expense report. Otherwise, a quick ques-
tion on the L.A. restaurant. . . .


Sincerely,
David Casnocha
```

>>

Start-up life is usually characterized by bootstrapping as much as possible. Anytime you can cut a corner, you try to, because one dollar less to an expense account means one more critical dollar to product development or sales. In the early goings your goal is to direct as much money as possible to those two areas (making the product better and then trying to sell the product), and as such, travel expenses, clothes, telephones, equipment, and fine cuisine fall by the wayside.

Being frugal is not as simple, though, as merely declaring "Spend less money." After all, *some* things demand fine quality: business cards, website, your deodorant. So figuring out when to cut and when to spend is the trick.

>>

At Comcate, the mandate to be frugal *and* raise sales *and* deliver a reliable product caused tensions in the company. One night, at 10:30 P.M., Dad stormed into my room.

For the first time in Comcate's history we were feeling a real cash squeeze. We had made significant investments in the early part of the year and our accounts receivable were dragging out. This instigated even more belt-tightening and questioning of expenses. Standing under my doorway Dad demanded an explanation of the L.A. trip I had scheduled the following day.

Brainstorm: Asking for Money
Versus Asking for Advice

The timeless start-up aphorism goes, "Never ask for money. Ask for advice instead, and you are more likely to get money. Never ask for free advice. Ask for money instead, and you'll get free advice."

In December 2003 Dave Richmond, Mike Patterson, Dad, and I visited Greg Prow again. When I first met Greg at Softbank/Mobius Venture Capital in 2001 I had an idea and early prototype. Now I returned with a full-time president, bushels of clients, real revenue, and lofty goals. We wanted to see if we were ready to raise venture money.

The second time around Greg invited two of his partners— Heidi Roizen and Brad Feld—to sit in. We ostensibly were "looking for money," but we wouldn't have known how to spend it if someone wrote us a check. What I really wanted was the opportunity to learn from these heavyweights. At the conclusion of the presentation, we asked if Mobius wanted to invest in Comcate. Heidi and Brad immediately started offering free advice (such as, don't raise money unless you absolutely need it). As the meeting transitioned from money to advice, I saw the opportunity to make the "big ask": "Would you guys introduce me to other entrepreneurs or possible mentors as I try to grow this business?" Both Heidi and Brad agreed enthusiastically and they've gone on to become important advisors, friends, and role models.

Sometimes, to get what you want, you have to ask for something different.

"How are you paying for the Southwest flight?"

"The Comcate credit card," I responded.

"OK, well, guess what? The company doesn't have any money!"

"True."

"We can't spend money frivolously."

"Well, Dad, how do you suggest we make it so the company *does* have money?"

Pause.

"Who's gonna bring in the sales?" I continued. "Are you? Are you doing pitches? Should we just sit back and wait for money to fall out of the sky?"

He pondered whether he should respond, but did not. He walked out of my room without saying another word.

I lay in bed shook up, at once unsure whether my trip to L.A. was worth the expense but also steadfast in my belief that we needed to sign up additional retired city managers to make introductions to potential clients.

I decided to cancel my L.A. trip.

First I called Southwest and cancelled my flight. Then I emailed my contacts and apologized and said I had a family emergency.

The next morning, having woken up after Dad left the house, I picked up a voicemail on my phone with the following apology. "Ben, I should have approached your L.A. trip differently, and I regret that you cancelled your plans," said my father.

>>

There are three lessons here for start-ups. First, it's necessary to be frugal. Dad's watchful eye helped the company enormously. Second, maintain open dialogue among everyone in the company about which kinds of expenses are tolerable in tight cash-flow situations. Everyone should feel empowered to challenge potentially frivolous expenses, but in a productive, organized way. Third, sometimes even when you think you need money to make life easier, you really don't. Just as long as you can put up with stained hotel carpets.

The Long, Hard Slog:
Achieving Scale

*Men wanted for hazardous journey. Small wages. Bitter
cold. Long months of complete darkness. Constant danger.
Safe return doubtful. Honour and recognition in case
of success.*
SIR ERNEST SHACKLETON

It's like the hamster whose exercise wheel never seems to stop. Or
the lecturer whose drone voice seems to freeze a classroom clock.
Or the hikers who unexpectedly encounter a mud swamp and
decide to trek by foot. Or, yes, even a new idea that has found roots
in the ground but seems to need endless water from its caretakers.
Every organization or person encounters what people term "growing pains"—the store whose products fly off the shelf every day, or
a teenager and puberty's surprises. But "growing pains" is far too
charitable a term for the phase of corporate growing up that this
chapter is about. Growing pains implies seam-bursting, pot-boiling,
eye-widening, CNBC-drooling growth. The long, hard slog, on the
other hand, allows for solid progress but at too slow a pace. You're
finished congratulating yourself on even getting to this stage—not
a shabby feat for a new idea—and are ready to focus on accelerating the sales, accelerating the product development, accelerating
the impact. The long, hard slog is what every person, idea, and
company must endure before they join the big leagues. Before they
can say without a wink that they are, in fact, "big."

>>

In a business, once you've discovered you have something and need to figure out how big of a something it is, your cocktail party buzzword manual probably instructs:

Tell new acquaintance: "My business has grown tremendously and now I'm really trying to, you know, really
trying to get some scale. We're trying to see if we can
scale the thing and become a massive company." Supplement
statement with hand gestures that mimic the volume of a
balloon as it is inflated with air.

Gartner calls this phase of growth "trough of disillusionment," but since five-syllable words like "disillusionment" can pose challenges to the avid wine-drinking schmoozer, most of us refer to it as the "long, hard slog." It means your company has some deals, but is generally doing less than $5M in revenue, and hasn't necessarily figured out how to surpass that level. I knew Comcate reached this stage when, starting in 2004, I heard the word "scale" more than any other in strategy meetings. At first it felt good. It's a club every company wants to join, after all, but not for too long. As in baseball everyone must touch first base, but no one wants to settle for just a single.

>>

Comcate had achieved good success selling our flagship eFM product to cities. We had paying customers, a working product, several hundred grand in recurring revenue, and a reasonably bustling sales pipeline. We had a full-time president, director of client services, and some basic infrastructure.[1] Our product was rock-solid. We had accumulated a tremendous wealth of domain expertise in the world of local government and IT. We had customers deploying our software across large organizations, integrating with complex technologies, and receiving international recognition for these efforts to boot. All this amounted to the gratifying conclusion that Comcate was *something*, and its premise had validity.

---

1 Dave was "promoted" to president from COO, which didn't mean anything but gave him the title he deserved. Titles are all about ego, but ego is not necessarily a bad thing.

But, how big could it be? The best entrepreneurs constantly raise the bar.

>>

The alternative to scaling Comcate would be to stay a "cash cow" and be self-sufficient. In this scenario we would remain a small company serving a modest number of clients and delivering a steady cash stream to our shareholders. This vision is not nearly as exciting, although it's less risky. More risk, more upside. If we concocted a plan to grow, we could raise additional investment and then increase our client base to several hundred government agencies. We wanted to go for it!

Prudently, before strategizing how we could accelerate growth we reflected on our successes to date—which meant confronting some disquieting truths. First, and most important, all of our sales wins took several customer meetings and phone calls, and several more such meetings to perform a successful implementation. For a $10,000- to $30,000-a-year product, the cost of sales—that is, the dollars we had to spend for the dollars we earned—was too high. Second, for all our basic infrastructure, we lacked an efficient marketing engine that could generate steady, qualified leads. Third, for all our domain expertise, local governments are truly local; that is, they all behave differently, making it hard to sell "expensive" software that would affect many people in an organization without a lot of consulting. All these discomforts were more than just challenges; they seemed like fundamental impediments to scaling our business. Or any business. What is your cost of sales? Do you have an efficient lead-generation system? Is each customer basically the same or is each unique?

>>

There are other questions companies ask themselves. For example, do we build scale or buy scale? Building scale means developing repeatable business processes (I know that sounds buzzword-ish) to grow the client base and revenue stream while preventing expenses from rising at the same rate. Most of the best companies achieve scale through organic growth, because a slow and steady march from ten clients to five hundred is often more manageable than instantly going from ten to five hundred, as is the case in a "buy" situation. When early-stage companies buy scale, they raise

Brainstorm: A Relationship-Based First Business

The factor that made Comcate successful early was relation-ship-based selling. *Relationship-based selling* means building personal connections with clients who can introduce you to their colleagues. Our sales cycle was long because of all the relationship-building that needed to transpire, but it was also remarkably effective—if you gave it time. But it's hard to *scale* a predominantly relationship-based business, which is why Comcate moved away from this model.

Regardless of whether it scales, it *is* a type of business that provides an extraordinary experience for the young execu-tive. It cultivates the skill of meeting someone, ropin' 'em in, creating mutual value, and then managing an interconnected group of relationships. These are skills that will surely outlast the life of the corporation. Compare these skills to those acquired in a less personal business: remote IT services, man-ufacturing, or even low-level positions in finance jobs. These kinds of businesses can be successful but may be less reward-ing for the entrepreneur in the long term.

I have met other young entrepreneurs who are much more successful than I am financially, but unless jealousy is shutting down my mental functions, I don't think they've developed the emotional and social intelligence that will help them in later careers.

If you want to start a business, think about judging its wor-thiness and ultimate success by metrics other than simple financial gain. The experience you gain developing critical life skills should certainly be high on the list. A people-inten-sive first business *can* be worth it.

---

financing to acquire other companies. In a fragmented market where several small players are competing for market share, the thinking goes, the winner is the company that can pull off a suc-cessful roll-up of all the other companies and become the trusted five-hundred-pound gorilla. The problem with buying scale is that it is deceptively simple. Most mergers and acquisitions fail.

>>

We wanted to grow organically.

Andy Sack, CEO of internet company Judy's Book, once posed on his blog three questions that every management team should ask themselves when struggling with growth:

1. What are the hardest problems in our current business approach—the issues we struggle over?
2. What's (surprisingly) easy about our business—the things that are working better than expected?
3. Where's the parade? What major trends are we trying to get in front of with our business?

At Comcate we decided that what was hard was selling an enterprise software product across a large organization. We decided what was easy was doing internet marketing and advertising to find new prospects from small cities. And the parade was forming around small agencies buying inexpensive software over the internet.

In light of these conclusions, our first decision involved our flagship product, eFeedbackManager. Our product was without doubt the best on the market for hosted CRM to small cities. The problems weren't with the product, they were with the market. Simply put, eFeedbackManager remained a nice-to-have, not a must-have.

"Some day, every city in America will need to have a system like this to track their communications. Yellow pads can only last for so long," I told Dave Richmond during the interview process in 2003.

It was now 2005 and that day had not yet come. Most cities were still making do with poorer alternatives. For the cities who *were* purchasing software like ours, there was still enough employee skepticism to make implementations lengthy and costly. There were also few barriers to entry in the market, allowing several new boutique firms to nab clients that should have been Comcate's.

When the product is a nice-to-have, the sales don't go fast enough. Period.

We conducted a variety of "tests" to see if we could bust through these challenges and shorten the sales cycle: we hired a retired city councilperson in West Virginia to try to sell the product as a reseller, we formed partnerships with other e-government providers, we attended different kinds of trade shows, and the like. None panned out. Sometimes, markets have a pace of their own and if your timing isn't right, there's little you can do to change it.

Our plan had to change. This is not unusual. It's exceedingly rare for a company to have the same business model a year after incorporation. As you learn, your plan *must* change.

>>

We turned our attention to what seemed easier. We had done some custom development for the City of Lancaster, California. At their request, we built a product for their Code Enforcement Division, the employees of which inspect neighborhoods for code violations such as eyesores, then issue citations and dole out fines. Not only was our code enforcement software mission-critical to their work and a smashing success in Lancaster, but other cities wanted it too.

By sheer accident we had developed a product that: (a) targeted a few people in the organization, therefore avoiding organization-wide buy-in pains, (b) required little ongoing maintenance and support, (c) had a relatively short sales cycle, and (d) met a critical need for the client.

Once we realized the significance of our success—selling a low-cost code enforcement product more or less over the internet, with little in-person assistance required—we aggressively introduced new kinds of modules to supplement it. We moved away from a vision of an expensive product suite for the entire enterprise, and instead toward the coming parade: a vision of targeted low-cost modules for cities, to be sold and delivered over the Web, that

---

Brainstorm: Getting More Good Revenue and Less Bad Revenue

All revenue is not made equally. When outsiders value your business they will consider different *kinds* of revenue.

When a company is trying to demonstrate its ability to scale its sales model it will face several trade-offs between "good" and "bad" revenue. Good revenue is obtained in a repeatable and efficient way. Winning the occasional RFP (request for proposals, the mechanism by which a government entity conducts a competitive bid) at Comcate does not contribute to proving that we can scale the sales predictably and cost-efficiently. Therefore, RFP deals, for us, are "bad revenue." On the other hand, signing up a client over the internet is cost-efficient, and therefore "good revenue."

If you start a bakery in town and convince the bank to loan you money based on a business model of selling baked goods to everyone in the neighborhood, and one day you drive into a different city and liquidate your remaining baked goods there, you have committed an "unnatural act." That is, you acted contrary to your stated vision, and while revenue is revenue, those generated by unnatural acts will be devalued by outsiders (unless the unnatural acts happen to be a better business model, in which case your vision must change). At Comcate our vision is to sell hosted, on-demand software (no CD-ROMs or on-site servers). Occasionally a client will request to host the software themselves at their office. If we agree to these terms, we do so reluctantly because we know this unnatural act will bring in bad revenue.

Bad revenue can really complicate an assessment of a company's performance. At one of our end-of-the-year wrap-up meetings, we reviewed our financials. As the board drilled into the revenue numbers, we spent an hour going deal by deal to figure out how each customer was acquired—by a "tight end," that is, slow and bulky and not scalable, or by a "wide receiver" or quickly, over the Web, and scalable. If there were too many tight-end deals we threw a yellow flag!

Most start-ups don't have the luxury of distinguishing between good and bad revenue. But for those that do, remember investors will give you more credit for "good revenue" and discount inflated revenue numbers that contain deals not compatible with your core, scalable model.

would meet distinct needs in often-overlooked agencies around the country. We continue to pursue this vision today.

>>

The "slog" in all this is the immense frustration that comes from the time it seems to take to figure out the strategy for growth and then act on it. Even in small, nimble companies, figuring out what's hard, what's easy, and where the parade is heading is trickier than it sounds. And it can take years to learn whether your bet for scaling the business will actually be the winning formula. You'd love instant feedback, but the market sometimes waits months before delivering a grade. At Comcate we tried a number of simultaneous "tests"—a new marketing approach, attending new conferences, a new referral system, different pricing—that each had different start and end dates. We tried to have as many hooks in the sea as possible to see which would catch, to see which would produce promising results.

>>

The long, hard slog is called that for a reason. Frustrating. Stressful. Never-ending. A grind. Slow. Repetitive. Board meetings start becoming a blur: "OK, we need to increase sales. We need to sign deals at a faster rate." Comcate was in the slog for more than a year.

It's at this stage of any new project when people are tempted to jump ship. In my experience it's not after an utter failure that people may leave—if they do, they can be labeled quitters—but it's during the slog. When progress seems ho-hum, when feedback from the market is ambiguous, when the light at the end of the tunnel is foggy. People are working hard but no matter how much sweat drips off their faces the train never seems to get moving fast enough. So they ditch.

It's the leader's job to stay focused and to emphasize process over results, patience over anxiety. This unwavering belief must be shared by all involved: if we make it through this stage, if we can prove a path to efficient growth, we will be a great company. And if being great were easy, after all, everyone would be great.

Brain Trust: Keep Slogging Away

BY CAROL RUTLEN

Be prepared for problems. Be prepared for setbacks. And be prepared for failure.

Start-ups by nature are risky ventures. If it was easy, you would have many competitors already dominating the market. A successful start-up is a blend of many elements—a need in the market, the right product, targeted messaging, successful selling, and great service. It is tough to get all those elements just right.

At my own software company, ExpatEdge, I endured the "long, hard slog" that Ben faced at Comcate. It's a natural stage in the entrepreneurial process and it's important to approach it with the right mindset.

No matter how clichéd, the most important piece of advice I remember during those tougher moments is: Don't give up. Keep slogging away. Listen to your customers. What are their concerns? Are you addressing their needs? Is your message getting across? Should you position your product differently?

Review your pricing. Is it too high? Or too low? How does it fit into your customers' budget? How does it compare to your competitors' pricing? Can you restructure the terms to make the price more acceptable?

Try different things. Could you sell your product to a different market? Or through another channel? How effective is your sales team?

And sometimes it just takes time—to establish a reputation in the marketplace, to build momentum, to build trust, or to lose the label of "just another start-up." Some markets have a natural pace that can be hard to accelerate.

Finally, remember that persistence pays off . . . eventually. As Thomas Alva Edison said, "Many of life's failures are people who did not realize how close they were to success when they gave up."

Carol Rutlen currently advises multinational companies on their stock plans and tax policy. She formerly ran ExpatEdge, a start-up software company.

Fulfilling the Mission, One Customer at a Time

Many persons have a wrong idea of what constitutes true happiness. It is not attained through self-gratification, but through fidelity to a purpose.
HELEN KELLER

Apple CEO Steve Jobs famously asked the then-Pepsi executive John Sculley in the mid-eighties, "Do you want to sell sugared water all your life or do you want to change the world?" Apple Computer is undoubtedly changing the world, but Comcate? The journey toward changing the world starts with a single person. . . .

>>

In late 2005 I received a phone call from Jack in Burgon Hills. If you recall, Jack was the resistant employee who didn't want to change his ways while I oversaw one of the first eFeedbackManager implementations. Jack had retired from Burgon Hills. In his free time he used his personal computer and the internet. And he found the internet a useful phenomenon.

"You know, it's pretty amazing. I'm using Yahoo! Finance to track my stocks and I can see exactly how complaints and questions could be tracked using technology too. I guess I didn't see the vision when you were describing it to me a few years ago. Now I do."

"Hey," I said, "I appreciate it. It means a lot. I just wish we could have counted you as an advocate at the city!"

"I know. I thought you would find this call . . . gratifying. But maybe frustrating at the same time. But I'm sure I'm not alone. You probably faced old people like me in other cities."

"We did."

"Well, that's what I wanted to say. Good luck . . . young man."

It was as if he had forgotten my name. It didn't matter. What mattered to Jack was that I was young and had a vision and he was old and now he saw it.

My conversation with Jack imparts a lesson for start-ups: timing counts. Sometimes your product won't work if you get to market too late—or too early. We may have been a little *ahead* of the curve in Burgon Hills.

>>

There are Jacks in all organizations around the country. Resistance to change will afflict *my* generation just as much as it has Jack's. Entrepreneurs must be the agents of change who implement disruptive products, convince tomorrow's skeptics of technology's potential for good, and propose to reinvent systems everyone else thinks are adequate. I can speak from experience: changing even small parts of people's everyday life, even if they're late adopters, is gratifying, but more important, it's a necessary step in changing the world in which we live.

>>

Jack's conversion to technology, while too late for Comcate to reap any gain, also crystallizes the lasting impact I hope my work will have on local government: turn slow-moving, old-school organizations into dynamic ones. Technology *can* transform their business. While writing this book I talked to several clients and they told me they expect eFeedbackManager to alter the DNA of their organization over the long term by making it more open, responsive, and internally efficient.

I founded Comcate to join the effort of making government less bureaucratic and more flexible, innovative, and entrepreneurial. For us, it's about improving the quality of life in the communities we serve by enriching the communication between

Brainstorm: Make Meaning: What Gets You and Your Employees Up Each Day?

I'm not a fan of lofty mission statements. Most have no meaning.

Guy Kawasaki, an author and speaker on entrepreneurship, once noted that companies should make a mantra—a short and sweet three- or four-word description of their goal in life—and then get on with it.

Comcate started with a nice-sounding but vague tagline: "Powering the Gov to Citizen Communication Link." Then we went to buzzword extreme: "Transforming Local Governments' Customer Interactions"—more accurate, but a mouthful.

Now, if someone asks me what Comcate does, I say, "We're trying to make local government more efficient and we're using technology to do it."

Make. Government. Better.

This kind of public service quality gets me up in the morning. It energizes me to talk to prospects and customers and try to help them get better at what they do best: provide an array of services to a diverse and demanding constituency.

Instead of trying to pack as many words as possible into a *typical* mission statement, be different. Think as much about what energizes you as about your business. What kind of legacy do you hope your company leaves in the world? What do your customers entrust in you? Try to boil this down into a handful of simple words and then let it evolve as your company grows.

citizens and their elected and appointed officials. We are a small piece of the make-the-world-a-better-place puzzle, but we're a piece nonetheless.

>>

Comcate doesn't just deliver software. We're powering the communication link from governments to their constituents. This larger vision and meaning behind Comcate—to transform the way government works—makes it an exciting place for our employees to work. Giving your business larger meaning is difficult, but the best companies capture the energy at the founding to create the necessary context for employees and customers.

At Comcate, we call this "fulfilling our mission—one agency at a time."

Me? I call this fulfilling *my* mission: to burn as brightly as possible for as long as possible by affecting lives and organizations in an enduring way.

Do you have a mission?

The Road Ahead:
Leaders of the Flat World

In times of change, learners inherit the Earth, while the
learned find themselves beautifully equipped to deal with
a world that no longer exists.
ERIC HOFFER

Each day is an opportunity to reinvent yourself. That means recon-
sidering who you are, what you stand for, and what you really want
to do in the world. Aren't some things supposed to stay steady in
good times or bad? No! *Always* rethink those questions. In my view,
you don't have a choice. The world is changing and you are dead
meat if you aren't constantly trying to make sense of the chaos.
Charles Darwin said, "It's not the strongest of the species that sur-
vives, nor the most intelligent, but the one most responsive to
change." In the next fifty years, we will see lots, and lots, and lots
of change.

As Comcate grows into the future, and as I look to create more
businesses, I think about the road ahead in the context of where I
will need to reinvent my skill sets to compete.

What will successful entrepreneurs have in common over the
next twenty years?

I humbly recommend entrepreneurs pay particular attention
to the following trends since I think they will define the future:

Globalization

This is a hot topic in the press, and for good reasons. We are witnessing greater interdependence throughout the world than ever before. Although globalization is not a new phenomenon, today's globalization is faster and more geographically dispersed. Some of the business implications are clear: more countries are participating in a global economy; decentralization trumps centralization; geographic distance between customers and employees means less; and certain jobs will be lost as new providers enter existing markets. Culturally, globalization alters the makeup of "national" cultures because global trade tends to produce a more synthetic variety. Local cuisine, fashion, and cultural identities will become more cosmopolitan.

Savvy entrepreneurs might respond to globalization in a few ways.

First, they will view the global marketplace as a source of opportunity. They will see educated workers from around the world as potential employees. They will see new and bigger customer markets in places such as China and India.

Second, they will commit to understanding global cultures. Working with an American is different from working with an Indian, which is different from working with a Brazilian. They will acknowledge that even as cultures and norms are brought closer together, diversity in thought processes will remain, and it will be up to someone to facilitate this melting pot.

Third, they will acquire solid foreign language skills and travel as much as possible.

Finally, they will advocate for sensible political policies that not only will make the entrepreneur's job easier but will increase the overall quality of life for most people in the world. In this spirit, they will reject protectionism, favor free markets, favor open immigration, and work to build social safety nets for those left behind.

Writing Skill

This may seem self-serving, since I enjoy writing, but I believe in it. Clear writing reflects clear thinking, and in an increasingly messy, complex world, clear thinking will be highly valued. Advanced math skills will be important for scientists and engineers—and we need more of those—but for an average businessperson I don't see math as integral to their future. Certainly a grounding in statistics and computation is important, and a strong grasp of accounting. But with the increasing speed and accessibility of computers, even basic math skills seem unnecessary in many kinds of jobs. So whereas technology will continue to process increasingly complex equations, I don't see technology being able to express increasingly complex ideas, or paint a literary picture, as good, human writing does. As entrepreneur and engineer Paul Graham has said, "Writing doesn't just communicate ideas; it generates them. If you're bad at writing and don't like to do it, you'll miss out on most of the ideas writing would have generated."

On-Demand Education

Due to globalization and accelerating change, knowledge—even of the most esoteric sort—is easily accessible. For example, one issue of the Sunday *New York Times* contains more information than somebody in the Middle Ages was exposed to in an entire lifetime. In the past, knowledge was scarce and you had to go to a university to acquire it. Now it's abundant, basically free, and at the mercy of the most curious. To stay sharp, the cutting-edge entrepreneur will take advantage of "on-demand" education and concede that the most important learning you do may occur *after* college or graduate school. As B. C. Forbes, founder of *Forbes* magazine, once said, "Vitally important for a young man or woman is, first, to realize the value of education and then to cultivate earnestly, aggressively, ceaselessly, the habit of self-education."

The other key implication of an abundant-knowledge society is the new emphasis on *experiences*. Experiences in the real world that apply learned knowledge will be valued more than ever. Knowledge may now be free, but experiences aren't. Entrepreneurs should acquire diverse experiences in different fields and countries so they can bring to bear a broader perspective than their competitors. Original thinking, especially in business, is rare. Couple common knowledge with uncommon experiences and you'll get ahead.

Nice Guys

In a connected world, reputation becomes transparent. Your reputation will follow you. Opinion websites, reputation networks, personal blogs, and the like all contribute to a more honest portrayal of somebody than anything available before. Thus, nice, likeable leaders win. Jerks will be exposed. No one wants to do business with an asshole. Sure, sometimes assholes win. But as Stanford professor Bob Sutton has said, "If you are a successful asshole, you are still an asshole and I don't want to be around you."

Be likeable and you'll win more often.

Brain Trust: How to Think About the Future

By Sean Ness

The keyboard taught me how to think about the future.

In seventh grade (in 1982), I learned to do a little BASIC programming. Though it didn't persuade me to become a programmer, I eventually decided to learn how to type by enrolling in a class with my best friend. I thought: computers will be big! We were the only guys in the class of forty, which led to a lot of ribbing from our buddies who questioned our manhood. But then our friends all took the class the next year, after seeing how critical computers were becoming.

What was so special about taking that typing class? Now that I work at the Institute for the Future, I understand that I was simply using a foresight-to-insight-to-action process. My foresight: computers would soon play a large role in the economy. This led to the insight that if I learned how to type, finding a computer-related job would be much easier. The action step was easy: learn to type!

In the age of the internet, everyone can know what is new, but only the best leaders will be able to sense what is important. Ben's story teaches us it's possible to create a meaningful business that rewards entrepreneurs who have foresight about coming trends.

Remember:

1. Develop foresight to sense and understand the context around the dilemmas that challenge you.

2. Develop your own insights and stimulate insights by others.
3. Learn when to act and how to learn from your actions.

What's today's keyboard? What's the foresight the best entrepreneurs have right now? I believe it's the ability to explore/analyze/synthesize abundant data. Driven by the unbridled increase in processing power, a new phrase is emerging: "simulation literacy." It will become more important than computer literacy. Information overload won't just be limited to bland Excel spreadsheets. You'll be dealing with high-resolution simulations (such as surgeons-in-training operating on lifelike mannequins) incorporating auditory, visual, and tactile inputs and outputs.

Sean Ness works at the Institute for the Future, the leading independent nonprofit research group that helps organizations make better, informed decisions about the future.

What Will You Be Shouting When You Reach the Grave?

To live is the rarest thing in the world. Most people exist, that is all.
OSCAR WILDE

In late August 2005 I returned to my high school. We seniors were off to our customary retreat before school started—two days in the Marin headlands. I felt refreshed and happy to see my friends again, some of whom I'd grown close to. During the summer I had worked for Comcate, but more interestingly, I left the country for the first time on a three-week exchange program in Zurich, Switzerland. I also read thirty books on all sorts of topics, and baked in the sun (I may be chairman of the board, but my tan is still important).

As my classmates and I boarded the big yellow school buses, I felt the familiar rub of my BlackBerry against my upper left thigh. After settling into a seat, I took off my BlackBerry, stuffed it into my backpack, and turned around to talk with my friends. We talked about the upcoming year and how fast time had flown. Then I turned and looked out the window. Fog, fog, fog wrapped the bus as we curved our way into the Marin hills. Time *had* flown. Just three years ago I had boarded the same bus to start high school, only at that time Comcate was in the midst of hiring an interim CEO, and I couldn't believe I would lose email access during the most critical phase.

The freshman year bus ride started two years of pure craziness. Twenty-five hours a week dedicated to my company, basketball during the winter, and a major social adjustment to the partying style of high school. *I've changed as a person*, I thought, by now the bus grinding on gravel, desperately climbing a hill. *I feel more self-confident than ever before.* I finally felt that when I represented myself in the adult business world I stood as a peer, not some kid. I finally felt that when I interacted with my school friends we developed deep rapport and mutual respect and shared (usually off-color) jokes. Finally.

>>

During my senior year of high school I applied to colleges. I had mixed feelings. On the one hand, I had and continue to have an intense desire to learn more, meet new kinds of people, and have my own ideas challenged. On the other hand, my mediocre academic experience in high school and own observations of college life didn't convince me that another four years of structured formal education would be effective. A meeting in New York with marketing author Seth Godin left me with the idea of the "real-life university." What kind of education would I receive if I spent four years traveling around the world, working, reading a hundred books a year, and meeting mentors? It was an intriguing alternative in the event that no traditional colleges appealed to me.

In my research I became dismayed at how many of the colleges, parents, counselors, and students fed into a mania that seemed so antientrepreneurial: standardized testing ad nauseam and endless babble about "resumes." Friends in private colleges also told me that in their $40,000-a-year institutions, booze trumped academic pursuit. An expensive way to live the life of the party!

Nonetheless, I did find some schools that seemed like exciting places to study academic subjects I'd never think about again, meet bright students from all over the world, and immerse myself in a new geography. I was a unique applicant to these liberal arts colleges and research universities due to my poor grades (2.6 GPA prior to senior year + 3.9 GPA first semester senior year = 2.99 cumulative GPA), decent SAT scores, and unusual extracurricular activities. No matter how compelling my other activities—editor-in-chief of the student newspaper, captain of the varsity basketball team, and then, of course, founding and operating Comcate—I knew that many colleges wouldn't look beyond the transcript. Even though they wouldn't appreciate the entrepreneurial experiences, I still did.

The more time that passes the happier I am I took the plunge my first two years of high school: starting a company, hiring programmers, signing up beta clients, hiring a president, growing the business, passing on the reins, working with media, engaging in broader Bay Area life, and so forth. As I told my college counselor, "I made choices, I don't regret them, and I'll accept the consequences."

I started visiting colleges that would appreciate my independent intellectual pursuits as worthy supplements to traditional classroom work. In the end I applied to a dozen schools and was thrilled to learn I had been accepted by most, including a small liberal arts college in Los Angeles County called Claremont McKenna College, a school devoted to "educating leaders in business and public affairs." I will enroll at Claremont in fall '07 after finishing my gap year. When it comes to government, public policy, and economics undergraduate education, Claremont has few equals and no superiors. Los Angeles will be a good base for me, and I won't mind the Southern California sunshine one bit.

>>

When I was a kid, some neighborhood friends and I would play tackle football at Kezar Stadium in San Francisco. I developed a reputation as a "bull." Despite being just ten years old, I would refuse to be tackled on a handoff, and it would take at least two guys four years my senior to bring me down, and even then I savored the dirt and mud that marred my face, as a reminder that bulls go down, and bulls get back up.

But sometimes I wouldn't hit the ground. My old basketball coach Darné used to scream at me if I made it through a whole basketball game without picking up a foul. "If you don't have a foul by the end of the game, you played too soft. You didn't take enough risks on defense," he said.

These are questions I often ask myself: Do I have dirt on my face? Have I picked up any fouls? Changing the world requires taking risks. You've taken a risk by reading this book. Are you ready to take another? Check out mystartuplife.com, if you are.

Brainstorm: Entrepreneurs Are Optimists

Have you ever met a pessimistic entrepreneur? I haven't.

Great entrepreneurs are what I call "cold water optimists." They're upbeat about the future, they believe they can *create* a better tomorrow, they believe that people are basically good, they believe hope inspires. But they are also practical—hence the "cold water" on their face that forces them to confront reality. They convert their optimism into tangible actions.

Newspaper headlines scream pessimism. Politicians and pundits can make a living off negativity. Cocktail parties are full of doomsayers, with optimists (especially young ones) written off as uneducated in the rough and unfair real world.

It's important for entrepreneurs to avoid these stains. Optimism opens the creative process for seeing the invisible. Optimism is the entrepreneur's flute—sweet and sometimes the lone voice, but it's what makes us different.

How can you, as an enterprising go-getter who sometimes faces a brutal reality, *build* optimism? In his book *Learned Optimism,* Martin Seligman argues that what distinguishes optimists and pessimists is their "explanatory style" of the events around them. If you aren't hired for that job, do you see this failure as permanent ("I'll never get another job") or as an isolated event? Do you incorporate this failure into your self-definition ("I'm just not smart enough to get a job") or as an incident for which there were probably many factors outside your control? Reflecting on how you explain things to yourself is the first step to becoming an optimist. Then, Seligman says, you should think about the usefulness of your pessimism (Is it getting you anywhere?), whether your pessimism withstands scrutiny of the evidence on which you base your negativity (Is it just irrational emotion?), and the implications of the unfortunate events (probably not as catastrophic as you make them out to be).

Remember—if you're still seeing the glass half-empty, go pour your glass of water into a smaller glass so it fills to the top!

We have reached the end. I hope I've shown how wonderful an entrepreneurial life can be, what some of the drawbacks or challenges are, and that only you can decide whether carving your own life path is Your Way. If you choose to join the legions of "life entrepreneurs," there will be people older *and* younger, side-by-side in the wonderful capitalist framework that is competition, working to effect change, working to make the world a better place.

>>

Mavis Leyrer once said, "The object of life's journey is not to arrive at the grave safely in a well-preserved body, but rather to skid in sideways, totally worn out, shouting, Holy shit, what a ride!!!"

What will you be shouting when you reach the grave?

Brain Trust: Let Your Heart Guide You

By Timothy J. Taylor

One of the first times I met Ben, we didn't sit in a conference room or at Starbucks. We met in a meditation garden off Union Street in San Francisco. We spent almost an hour talking about the essence of leadership and passion without explicitly discussing business.

That afternoon we talked about the light of love inside all of us. This conversation revealed qualities of Ben I gravitate toward: honesty, humor, intelligence, and attentiveness to others. Since then, Ben and I have had numerous discussions about soul and spirit and its relevance in the competitive, fast-paced world of entrepreneurship.

I've learned that the material success in business Ben and I enjoy is temporary (that is, you can't take it with you). This realization has been critical to both our lives. And having worked with hundreds of entrepreneurs, I find it's been critical to others as well—the most successful ones know that no matter how much money they make, true peace is eternal and achieved from within.

In your start-up or your career, you will be faced with challenges that will frustrate and confuse you. You will experience material successes or failures—let your heart guide you.

If you look at the best leaders in business I think you'll find they're too busy *living* to worry about material wealth. Material success is a by-product of a focus on their total well-being. Ben and I live it. You can live it too.

Timothy J. Taylor connects entrepreneurs with investors and customers in Silicon Valley. He also is the oral presentation coach for all the entrepreneurs who pitch the Band of Angels investment group.

Appendix A: What's Next

I spent a long, long time on this book. And with the way the publishing world works, I probably won't make much money on it. I wrote it because I believe in the power of each of us to change the world. So I only ask of you one thing: *begin*. Get started. "Live in life," as Joan Didion would say. Go start a company. Go start a club. Create a website, write a blog, cold-call your hero. Buy this book for your friends and talk about it. Talk about entrepreneurship. Read more books. But *start*. *Now*. The clock is ticking. If not now, when? If not you, who?

I'm ready to help.

Tap into a larger community around *My Start-Up Life* by visiting the companion website: www.mystartuplife.com. There you will find additional content and be able to connect with fellow readers. You can sign up for my email newsletter or subscribe to my blog.

If you need a little more, turn the page to find a one-a-day vitamin plan!

Appendix B: A One-a-Day, One-Month Plan to Becoming a Better Entrepreneur

It's time to get started. Here are some daily vitamins designed to be digested one per day. Over the next month focus on each of these items for a full day—how can they become habits for *you*? If you're looking for even more, log onto mystartuplife.com and find additional suggestions around each of the ideas with an *online* label.

Day 1. *Meet as many people as you can.* Be open to randomness when meeting new people. In New York, the person waiting your table could be the next big movie star. Apply a "Who knows?" mentality to every encounter. After you meet someone, be meticulous in your organization and follow-up.

Day 2. *Start reading.* You are what you read. Read magazines, newspapers, books, blogs, websites. All knowledge is accessible. The most curious win. *Online: Find specific magazines and books you should read.*

Day 3. *Email five people you'd like to meet, but don't know yet.* You never know until you try. You'll be surprised how many people will write back.

Day 4. *Become a top-notch emailer.* Get good at filtering emails and managing the inflow. Be careful before "Replying All." Answer *all* email promptly. Figure out how to become even more productive. Here's a tip: if you can answer it in under a minute, do it now.

Day 5. *Write down everything.* When you move at the speed of an entrepreneur, it's easy to forget things. Write down your ideas, your to-do's, your notes from the meeting. Organize them. *Online: Learn how to organize your fringe thoughts.*

Day 6. *Become a sophisticated listener.* Try to discern hidden meanings. Develop a reputation as someone who can listen to other peoples' issues in a compassionate, genuine way.

Day 7. *Send five handwritten notes.* Think about five people who mean a lot to you and mail them a handwritten note, right now, expressing your appreciation. *Online: Each handwritten note should be four lines long.*

Day 8. *Create an expert effect.* Develop expertise in an issue that others will find valuable. Become an indispensable resource in *something.*

Day 9. *Travel somewhere.* Get outside your normal frame of reference and see what happens. See if you approach an issue with a new perspective. See if a new physical place puts you in a new mental place. Make a reservation today! *Online: See the best places to visit.*

Day 10. *Raise the bar for one day and observe results.* Hold impeccable standards for one full day. No crappy emails, no half-ass efforts, no tasks put off, no workout skipped, no silly indulgence in unhealthy food. Easier than you thought?

Day 11. *Read* The Kite Runner *along with Jack Welch's* Straight from the Gut. See which you find more interesting. *Online: Find other nonbusiness books that will rock your world.*

Day 12. *Research charities, give money, and then talk to your friends about why you did it.* Tune your antenna to causes that excite you. *Online: Find out about charities that are changing the world.*

Day 13. *Build a smart "personal finance infrastructure."* Start saving money. Invest in index funds. Keep and track a budget. Get wealthy. *Online: Personal finance 101.*

Day 14. *Write a blog.* Put yourself out there. Share your ideas. Disclose yourself. Become transparent. *Online: How to start a blog and which blogs to read.*

Day 15. *Pour your heart into it.* Say what you mean and mean what you say. Total enthusiasm—straight from the heart—in all efforts.

Day 16. *Form an advisory board.* Surround yourself with bigger souls and sharper brains.

Day 17. *Find someone younger/less experienced than you and help them.* Give a little, get a lot back. Not only will you learn a ton, it will feel good, too.

Day 18. *Be religious with a to-do list.* If it doesn't go on a task list, it doesn't get done.

Day 19. *Stop watching TV.* If you do, "I don't have time" will always ring false.

Day 20. *Find your pole.* Life gets crazy sometimes. We all need to swing around something. For some, religion is their pole. Find your pole, your steadying center influence, and never lose sight of it.

Day 21. *Know what you don't know.* Figure out what you're good at and find others who help you where you're not. Reduce your blind spots as much as possible. *Online: See how to reduce your blind spots.*

Day 22. *Make someone call you an asshole.* You don't know where a line exists until you cross it. Be brash and overly confident until someone says, "Stop being such an asshole." That's when you've crossed the line. Take four or five steps back, and then you're in the right place.

Day 23. *Be quick, but don't hurry.* Sometimes you'll need to sprint. But business can be a marathon. Markets—and life—have a natural pace. Be quick within that framework.

Day 24. *Keep a stash of positive thoughts handy.* Positive affirmations go a long way. Here's one: "Just trust yourself. Then you will know how to live." *Online: Find other positive thoughts.*

Day 25. *Hold fewer meetings.* Talk less, act more. *Online: Learn how to run and participate in excellent meetings.*

Day 26. *Act on incomplete information.* Former U.S. Joint Chiefs of Staff Chairman Colin Powell expected his commanders in the field to make decisions when they had 40 percent of the potentially available information. In life-or-death situations. And you think you need more information?!

Day 27. *Set up a virtual office.* Search for "Web 2.0 applications" online and start implementing tools to make you a mean, lean, virtual machine. *Online: Tools that will make you lean and mean are available.*

Day 28. *Have multiple side projects going.* Diversify your portfolio of interests and activities.

Day 29. *Be funny.* Humor can be scarce in a serious world. Be that guy people want to be around. Research humor and good one-liners. *Online: Funny business: humor for the busy executive.*

Day 30. *Make people feel like a million bucks.* It all starts with people. Here's a tip: if you're going to compliment someone, do it in public.

Appendix C: Ben's Reading List

I'm a bookslut. I undress my unread bookshelf with my eyes and imagine myself buried in the books' dark, curvy lines of black text. Books are a source of entertainment and learning for me. There are good nonfiction books on virtually every topic imaginable, and some six thousand new business books are published each year. I'll read some fiction now and then, but only by the best (Tom Wolfe, Philip Roth, and the like). For businesspeople I recommend that at most three or four of every ten books you read should be conventional "business books." Books outside the realm of traditional business can be surprisingly rewarding and helpful. Here are my top picks.

Business
Crossing the Chasm, by Geoffrey Moore
The Ultimate Question, by Fred Reichheld
Winning the Loser's Game, by Charles Ellis
The Moral Consequences of Economic Growth, by Benjamin Friedman
The MouseDriver Chronicles, by Kyle Lusk and John Harrison
Freakonomics, by Steven Levitt and Stephen Dubner
The Effective Executive, by Peter Drucker
Soros: The Life and Times of a Messianic Billionaire, by Michael Kaufman
The Medici Effect, by Frans Johanson
Free Prize Inside and the Big Moo, by Seth Godin
Softwar: An Intimate Portrait of Larry Ellison, by Matthew Symonds
The Marketing Playbook, by John Zagula
How Would You Move Mount Fuji? by William Poundstone
The Four Obsessions of an Extraordinary Executive, by Patrick Lencioni
The Entrepreneur's Guide to Business Law, by Constance Bagley
Good to Great, by Jim Collins
On Becoming a Leader, by Warren Bennis

Information Rules, by Carl Shapiro and Hal Varian
eBoys, by Randal Stross
Fooled by Randomness, by Nassim Nicholas Taleb
Compassionate Capitalism, by Marc Benioff
Love Is the Killer App, by Tim Sanders

Globalization
The World Is Flat, by Tom Friedman
Creative Destruction, by Tyler Cowen
Globaloney, by Michael Veseth
Money Makes the World Go Round, by Barbara Garson
How "American" Is Globalization? by William Marling

Intellectual Life
The Blank Slate, by Steven Pinker
The Presentation of Self in Everyday Life, by Erving Goffman
Reflections by an Affirmative Action Baby, by Stephen Carter
Integrity, by Stephen Carter
The Accidental Asian, by Eric Liu
Mind Wide Open, by Steven Johnson
Socrates Café, by Chris Phillips
Self-Renewal, by John Gardner
Public Intellectuals, by Richard Posner

Psychology
Influence: The Psychology of Persuasion, by Robert Cialdini
Flow, by Mihaly Csikszentmihalyi
Man's Search for Meaning, by Viktor Frankl

Biography/Memoir
My Life, by Bill Clinton
This Boy's Life, by Tobias Wolff
Swimming Across, by Andy Grove
All Over But the Shoutin', by Rick Bragg
Personal History, by Katherine Graham
Emerson: Mind on Fire, by Robert Richardson
In an Uncertain World, by Robert Rubin
The Year of Magical Thinking, by Joan Didion

Religion
End of Faith, by Sam Harris
The Universe in a Single Atom, by the Dalai Lama

The World's Religions, by Huston Smith
The Bhagavad-Gita
Plan B: Further Thoughts on Faith, by Anne Lamott
Under the Banner of Heaven, by Jon Krakauer

Politics/Current Affairs

Ghost Wars, by Steve Coll
Running the World, by David Rothkopf
Founding Brothers, by Joseph Ellis
A Conflict of Visions, by Thomas Sowell
Going Nucular, by Geoffrey Nunberg
America at the Crossroads, by Francis Fukuyama
Holidays in Hell, by P. J. O'Rourke
River Town, by Peter Hessler

Novels

I Am Charlotte Simmons, by Tom Wolfe
Reading in the Dark, by Seamus Deane
Dubliners, by James Joyce
The Scarlet Letter, by Nathaniel Hawthorne
The Plot Against America, by Philip Roth
Ender's Game, by Orson Scott Card
Disgrace, by J. M. Coetze
Indecision, by Benjamin Kunkel
The Secret Life of Bees, by Sue Monk Kidd
The Bonfire of the Vanities, by Tom Wolfe
Saturday, by Ian McEwan

Random

On Paradise Drive, by David Brooks
How to Be Alone, by Jonathan Franzen
A Hope in the Unseen, by Ron Suskind
Dress Your Family in Corduroy and Denim, by David Sedaris
Clinton & Me, by Mark Katz
What Does It Mean to Be Well Educated? by Alfie Kohn
Consider the Lobster, by David Foster Wallace
A Supposedly Fun Thing I'll Never Do Again, by David Foster Wallace

Acknowledgments

I am lucky on many levels, and it's most evident if I think about the people who have entered my life.

My family has provided an endless well of support and love: Dad, Mom, John, and Alex.

Thanks to the early customers of Comcate: Bud Ovrom and Vida Tolman, Mike Ramsey, Audrey Seymo

Many individuals have positively affect
ful for the light they have shined on me. A
Russell Anam, George Baker, Marc Benio
Besselo, Ori Brafman, Bill Bullard, Kai Ch
Valerie Cunningham, Jackie Danicki,
Durand, Terry Duryea, Brad and Amy
Catherine Hutton, Nasif Iskander, Carl
Richard Kassissieh, Greg Lahann, Tom Lewcock, Seth Levine; Chris Wand, Jason Mendelson, and Ryan McIntyre at Mobius VC; Kirk Lorie, Olivier Marchand, Anthony More, Tom Mulvaney, Matt Palmquist, Jeff Parker, Mike Patterson, Greg Prow, Jon Reider, Dave Richmond, Heidi Roizen, Carol Rutlen, Chris Sacca, Ramit Sethi, Max Shapiro, the Siegrist family, Steve Silberman, Darren Stowell, Jon Swartz, Tim Taylor, Trevor Traina, Mark Waters (and the Water-Ware Internet Services team), Chris Yeh, and Bill Zaner.

My friends from school are amazing people. Some friends who have been important to me at different times of my life include: Dario Abramskiehn, Jeremy Avins, Elena Butler, Ted Conrad, Patrick Free, Conrad Hendrickson, Andrew Hess, Mack Howell, Mike Ketcham, Jason Kwok, David Lee, Andy McKenzie, Kevin Mira, Natty Pachtner, Danielle Robin, Ben Springwater, Howard Swig, Austin Tyler, Lincoln Wheeler, and Sam Williams.

I have many anonymous readers of my blog from around the world and I thank them for indulging me, critiquing me, and following along in real-time in this adventure.

The team at Jossey-Bass/Wiley made this book a reality. Neal Maillet offered warmth, professionalism, and a vision. Various friends reviewed this manuscript along the way and undoubtedly made it much stronger: Peter Economy, Jesse Berrett, Barbara Smith, Mike Patterson, Dave Richmond, Chris Yeh, Ramit Sethi, Rahim Fazal, Heidi Roizen, Rob Urstein, Tim Taylor, Emily Casnocha, David Cowan, and most especially, David Casnocha.

There are many others who deserve ink. This book is only possible because of all of you; however, any fallacies or misrepresentations in the book are my fault alone.

Endnotes

All URLs that appear here are linked to my website for easy access: www.mystartuplife.com. Some of the URLs may have changed over time.

Introduction
The Apple Computer "Think Different" TV advertisement is available at http://www.youtube.com/watch?v=KreJkItCk4E.
The Joan Didion quote is from her commencement address titled "Looking Out" on June 15, 1975, at the University of California, Riverside.

Chapter 1.0: My Dot-Com Life Begins
The title and part of the idea for the sidebar "Who Knows What Could Happen If You Raise Your Hand?" came from Ramit Sethi at http://www.iwillteachyoutoberich.com/archives/2006/07/ramit_teaches_kids_bribes_them.html.

Chapter 2.0: Nature or Nurture?
References to "Flow" in "All the Fuss About 'Passion'—and How to Tap into Yours" are based on Mihaly Csikszentmihalyi in *Flow: The Psychology of Optimal Experience* (New York: HarperCollins, 1990).
The statistic on rebate fulfillment comes from ConsumerAffairs.com, cited at http://www.youngmoney.com/consumer/shopping_tips/060401.

Chapter 3.0: The First Axiom of Business
The term "fringe thoughts," used in the sidebar "The Fringe-Thoughts List: Where Most Great Ideas Develop," was coined by C. Wright Mills in his book *The Sociological Imagination* (Oxford: Oxford University Press, 2000).

Chapter 5.0: First Meeting with a VC
The phrase "red sugary buzz . . . each an expression of the other" was inspired by a passage in Benjamin Kunkel's excellent novel *Indecision* (New York: Random House, 2005), p. 39.

The article mentioned in "The Power of Mentors" is G. R. Roche, "Much Ado About Mentors," *Harvard Business Review,* 1979, *1,* 14–31. See http://careerfocus.bmjjournals.com/cgi/content/full/324/7353/ S203#B3.

Chapter 6.0: Signing Up Early Customers

The Southwest Airlines CEO quote mentioned in the sidebar "I Have a Strategic Plan. It's Called Doing Things," as well as the idea of action, came from Tom Peters's slides: "111 Ridiculously Obvious Thoughts on Selling." See http://www.tompeters.com/slides/ uploaded/Sales111_012806.pdf.

Some tips in "Asking Questions: There's a Right and a Wrong Way" are drawn from "The Question Man," by Susan Paterno, *American Journalism Review,* Oct. 2000; see http://www.ajr.org/article_printable. asp?id=676.

Chapter text asks the follow-up question, "Why did you ask that question?" This sales technique comes from Chris Yeh; see http://chrisy eh.blogspot.com/2006/08/why-do-you-ask.html.

Chapter 7.0: Confronting Failure . . . and Bouncing Back

I cite William Davidow's *Marketing High Technology* (New York: Free Press, 1986).

Chapter 8.0: Hiring an Interim CEO

The sidebar "Three Sure Ways to Maximize Luck" appeared first, under my byline, in *Youth Wealth: Trade Secrets from Teens Who Are Changing American Business,* by Jon Swartz (Bloomington: Rooftop Publishing, 2006). The idea of "exposing yourself to randomness" comes in part from Brad Feld during a personal conversation on the value of traditional four-year universities (home to random events, speakers, and activities). The idea of "self-deception" comes from Dan Gilbert in his book *Stumbling on Happiness* (New York: Knopf, 2006).

Chapter 9.0: The Hunt for a COO

I quote Jim Collins's *Good to Great* (New York: HarperCollins, 2001).

The sidebar "How to Overcome Fear of Failure" mentions "self-protection." This idea comes from an online exchange between ESPN's Bill Simmons and *New Yorker* writer Malcolm Gladwell; see http:// proxy.espn.go.com/espn/page2/story?page=simmons/060302.

Text references to Microsoft's interview questions come from *How Would You Move Mount Fuji?* by William Poundstone (Boston: Little, Brown, 2003).

Chapter 10.0: Life as a Road Warrior

I cite Geoffrey Moore's *Crossing the Chasm* (New York: HarperBusiness, 1999) and Cliff Atkinson's *Beyond Bullet Points* (Seattle: Microsoft Press, 2005).

Chapter 11.0: I'm a Sophomore

The main ideas developed in the sidebar "Being a Corporate Athlete" came from the book *The Power of Full Engagement,* by Jim Loehr and Tony Schwartz (New York: Simon & Schuster, 2003).

The text on academic struggles mentions childhood versus adult precociousness. This idea came from an article in the Association for Psychological Science's *Observer;* see http://www.psychologicalscience. org/observer/getArticle.cfm?id=2026.

The same text section discusses the desire to be appreciated for effort. This idea appeared in early drafts of my book, and Malcolm Gladwell recently discussed it on his own blog: http://gladwell.typepad.com/ gladwellcom/2006/09/degree_of_diffi.html.

I cite Erving Goffman's *Presentation of Self in Everyday Life* (New York: Anchor, 1959).

Chapter 12.0: A Silicon Valley Life

"Networking 101" and "Networking 202" contain ideas from my friend Auren Hoffman.

"Creating and Projecting Brand 'Me'" contains some ideas discussed in the e-book by Rajesh Setty on personal branding; see http://www. lifebeyondcode.com/ebooks/PBTP.pdf.

I cite Marc Benioff and Carlye Adler's *The Business of Changing the World* (New York: McGraw-Hill, 2006).

Chapter 13.0: The Product Development Process

The sidebar "Dare to Be Mediocre: Good Is the Enemy of Perfect" contains ideas by Auren Hoffman.

Chapter 15.0: The Long, Hard Slog

The reference to Gartner, Inc.'s "trough of disillusionment" and the kind of company that gets stuck in the long, hard slog comes from my friend Seth Levine on his blog: http://sethlevine.typepad.com/ vc_adventure/2006/01/when_should_you.html.

Andy Sack's blog post on "three questions each management team should ask themselves" is at http://asack.typepad.com/a_sack_of_seattle/ 2006/10/the_meeting_tha.html.

"Getting More Good Revenue and Less Bad Revenue" is based on an idea
discussed on Will Price's blog: http://www.willprice.blogspot.com/
2006/09/how-pure-is-your-model.html.

Chapter 16.0: Fulfilling the Mission, One Customer at a Time

The sidebar "Make Meaning" contains ideas from Guy Kawasaki's top ten
start-up rules; see http://www.alwayson-network.com/printpage.
php?id=11962_0_11_0_C.

Chapter 17.0: The Road Ahead

I cite Paul Graham's essay "Writing Briefly," available at http://www.
paulgraham.com/writing44.html.

Chapter 18.0: What Will You Be Shouting When You Reach the Grave?

"Entrepreneurs Are Optimists" contains ideas from *Learned Optimism,* by
Martin Seligman (New York: Vintage Books, 2006).

The Author

Ben Casnocha (pronounced kas-NO-ka) is a Silicon Valley–based entrepreneur and writer. Currently nineteen years old, he serves on the board of Comcate, (pronounced KOM-kate) Inc., the leading e-government technology firm he founded six years ago. He has received various accolades. In 2006 *BusinessWeek* named him one of America's best young entrepreneurs. In 2004 PoliticsOnline ranked him among the "twenty-five most influential people in the world of internet and politics." The *Silicon Valley Business Journal* named his blog one of the "Top 25 in Silicon Valley." His work has been featured in hundreds of media around the world, including CNN and *USA Today.* He is a seasoned speaker on entrepreneurship and leadership, and he cofounded an intellectual discussion society for business and technology executives. He graduated from San Francisco University High School in June 2006, where he edited the school newspaper and was captain of the varsity basketball team. While writing this book in a "gap year," he traveled to nearly twenty countries, staying at the homes of his blog readers, and also worked for three months at a venture capital firm. He enrolls at Claremont McKenna College in September 2007.

His website is www.mystartuplife.com.